THE VOICE OF INTUITION

Write from the Heart

About the Author

Emily Chantiri is a best selling author and journalist. She is a regular contributor to a number of leading publications, including the Sydney Morning Herald, The Australian Financial Review and BRW Magazine. She is also the author of four books, including two bestsellers, The Money Club, Financially Fit for Life. Her book, The Savvy Girl's Guide to Money has been translated and sold into several countries. Chantiri lives in Sydney.

She can be found online at www.emilychantiri.com and www.thevoiceofintuition.com

Emily's other books include:

The Money Club - *Random House*
Financially Fit for Life - *Random House*
Everyday is Mother's Day - *Wiley Books*
The Savvy Girl's Money Book - *Allen and Unwin*

All rights reserved. No part of this publication may be reproduced or transmitted in any form or by any means, electronic or mechanical, including photocopying, without written permission of the publisher.

National Library of Australia Cataloguing-in-Publication Data
ISBN 978-0-9875637-0-5

© 2013 Emily Chantiri

Cover design by Daniel Churches; www.dchurches.com.au

Cover photo: Myrtle Beach, South Carolina, USA

Contents

About the Author	i
Acknowledgments	iv
Foreword by Katrina Cavanough and Tony Crisp	vi
Introduction	x
Preface	xviii
Chapter 1: Myrtle, Myrtle	1
Chapter 2: Intuition	9
Keeping a Dream Journal	*14*
Chapter 3: Karen and Bali	17
How to Use Oracle Cards	*26*
Chapter 4: Vera	27
Understanding Chakras	*37*
Chapter 5: A Hawaiian Storm Before the Dream	39
Chapter 6: Robert	45
Chapter 7: The Unravelling of Myrtle	53
Chapter 8: The Dream Becomes a Reality	59
Chapter 9: On the Road to Myrtle Beach	65
Chapter 10: Another Dream: Shantaram	71
Chapter 11: Myrtle Beach and the Golfing Mecca	77
Chapter 12: The Meher Spiritual Retreat	83
Chapter 13: Janine	87
Chapter 14: Another Myrtle!	91
Chapter 15: What is Intuition?	99
How Does Intuition Work?	*101*
Chapter 16: Memories of Myrtle	107
Chapter 17: Thirteen Days and Another Revelation	111
Chapter 18: The Silent Voice	115
Chapter 19: Getting Back to Normal	119
Chapter 20: Life Goes On	121
APPENDIX	124

Acknowledgments

This book has been a labour of love for me to write. There are a number of people I have to thank for encouraging me to continue to the end. First and foremost a big heartfelt thanks to, Jennifer Rose, Jackie Nugara, Sylvia Percival and Kerryn Fisk and finally to my family; my siblings, my sons and my partner.

This book is dedicated to
the inner voice in all.

Foreword by Katrina Cavanough

Intuition is often misunderstood and understandably so. It can be challenging to describe and unless we are open to hearing its soft whispers and feeling its strong urges then it can be mistaken or worse, dismissed.

On the other hand, when harnessed it can be a great internal compass that helps us navigate a clear course as we move through life. The greatest misunderstanding is the myth that intuition is only available to a select few of 'gifted people'. These people are seen to have some special power or talent that sets them apart from others in their community. Sadly this leads to many people believing they cannot access this part of themselves as they perceive it is not there. They live their lives unaware of this great resource that is available to them.

In The Voice of Intuition Emily has broken through these misunderstandings and returned the way we see intuition back to the everyday in a most powerful way. Through her own story we can see that listening to your inner voice will take you on the greatest journey and will always deliver you to the correct destination.

Bravely, Emily trusts her own intuition and as she does a great adventure begins to unfold. Driven by a desire to uncover the mystery of a prophetic dream she travel across the globe to learn of a spiritual leader whose message so happens to be about the power of the inner voice.

Emily weaves a simple yet powerful message through an intriguing story about her own relationship with intuition. Emily shows us so well that it is the message that rests within yourself, that gives you the most reliable answer. It is the same for everyone.
Resting within the pages are practical tools offering everyday strategies to discover and strengthen your intuition. These tools transformed this book from an inspirational story into a powerful resource that will completely change your life.
As I read The Voice of Intuition I felt a deep sense of relief wash over

me. I understand now why I was asked to write the foreword. Emily's experience of intuition was much the same as my own. She lived in the real world and in her life she naturally used all her senses. There was no fuss about it. But she listened and she was rewarded.

It is time for these stories, and others like it, to be told. Grand adventures spurred on by prophetic dreams and guided by a strong inner compass. A story told with a style and personality that only a journalist could offer. Grounded. Matter of fact. Real, everyday life.

Emily's story will take you on the most grand adventure. As you travel along the way with her don't be surprised if you feel inspired to listen more closely to your own inner voice. As you do you will reconnect with all of who you are including your intuition.

Katrina Cavanough, author of Wisdom For Your Life (Allen & Unwin)
Speaker, Author, Exceptional Life Guidance
www.katrinacavanough.com

Foreword by Tony Crisp

Dreams are one of the main doorways to our inner life. Emily's book is a great statement to the wonder of such insight. Not being a textbook makes it an interesting read right to the end.

Dreams and intuition is a doorway to the infinite resources of the human spirit. The important questions of our life are the things that prompt our intuitive responses. Emily's work, along with her courageous approach to life, and her loving spirit, were door openers for her. But in fact any aspect of life can be a way of gaining insights through this great gift. The famous neurologist Dr. Shafica Karagulla found that many doctors use their intuition as a means of knowing what is really wrong with their patients. Also Edgar Cayce could answer any question put to him via his amazing intuition.

Emily's intuitive gift led her to slowly extend her ability of writing and encouraged her to go beyond her old self, find love, and also a path which promises to extend her life into the new and fascinating. I feel sure this extension of her gifts will lead her to write another book – an even more fascinating one.

Tony Crisp, author of international best seller, the Dream Dictionary.

Introduction

Like many Australians, I was raised in an average family from a multicultural background. I am the eldest of six children: five girls and one boy. As you can imagine, with this number of children in one household, there were many fights. We usually fought in pairs: My brother and I would fight with each other, and then my next two sisters would fight, and then the youngest two. We fought hard and often. We'd scream and yell at each other, particularly when one sibling took something that belonged to the other. We still loved each other, but with so many children growing up in a small, modest home, fights were bound to happen. It's embarrassing to me now as I think back to the way we fought, because today we get on so well.

My parents migrated in the early '60s from Lebanon to Australia. At the time, Australia was in need of skilled workers. An immigration campaign resulted in extensive international recruitment to bring in new workers. My dad had a knack with cars. He was a great mechanic, and later in his career, he repaired aeroplane engines, too. This skill was his ticket to Australia.

I envied my dad's ability to speak four languages: Lebanese, English, French and some Italian. He was a staunch Catholic—hence, the number of children. We were just like any other large family growing up in suburban Sydney. Our home was a typical weatherboard cottage with three bedrooms. Later, when more kids came along, my parents added an extra room. We knew our neighbours, and they knew us. In their eyes, we were a nice family. To my surprise, we often received comments about how attractive our family was. I wasn't so sure about this. My sisters and I were not the typical blue-eyed blondes, which was the definition of beauty during the '70s and '80s. However, I still recall how we all received plenty of comments about our eyes. "How lucky you are to have those long lashes and big eyes," our neighbours would say.

My mother was the family rock, and she was the most amazing cook. Everything she made was a hit, especially her tabbouli and hummus, and not just with the immediate family but also with all of our friends, our extended family and even our neighbours. No wonder they liked us! My mother could happily feed the whole street at a moment's notice.

It was no surprise, then, that as a teenager I was fat. It's hard for people who know me today to believe this, because I am much slimmer now, but I was definitely overweight, and it was because of my mother's delicious food. After school, I would race home and dive into the feast that she had prepared for us. On a typical day, she would cook stews, stuffed eggplant (my favourite), pastas, marinated olives and pickles, fresh Lebanese bread and Lebanese sweets (my other weakness). No wonder I was overweight! My sisters were all slightly overweight, too, but thankfully, we have all trimmed down now that we're older.

As well as being an amazing cook, my mother worked to ensure we had everything we needed. She was the kindest woman I have ever met. Nothing would please her more than welcoming visitors into our home. She loved whipping up her amazing dishes and feeding people. We were never short of visitors—or food!

Growing up in Sydney's inner western suburbs meant that many nationalities surrounded us. As well as mixing with people of Lebanese origin, my parents had friends who were Italian, French, Australian and Croatian. I felt we were very lucky to have such a colourful assortment of people in our lives. I believe this diverse mix of people helped pique my interest in people and cultures. As a writer and journalist, my favourite assignments are those about people.

At school, I didn't perform particularly well, and I didn't get good grades. I was not one of the bright kids. In fact, I'd go so far as to say that I was invisible to most teachers; quite a few of them couldn't even remember my name! That's how average I was. I loved art, English and history, and my grades reflected some talent in those subjects, but by no means was I a stand-out student. However, it was my love of English and art that led me to become a writer.

Looking back at my teenage years, it's hard to believe that I was painfully shy. That shy teenager has gone on to write books, has appeared on television and spoken on radio, and has even interviewed a few well-known personalities!

Thanks to my job as a journalist, I have met and interviewed some of the most fascinating people, not only in Australia but also across the world. I've interviewed many of the country's wealthiest business people, from fashion designer Peter Morrissey and international make-up guru Napoleon Perdis to mining magnate Andrew Forrest and world-renowned human behaviourist Dr John Demartini. Yes, journalism has given me access to powerful people and exciting destinations, but I still insist that I live a very ordinary and normal life.

I spent the years living at home with my parents helping my mother and looking after my siblings. When I wasn't helping out, my one passion was to draw. I was a very creative child. My parents didn't understand my love of drawing and painting and thought it was trivial. They expected me to help around the house, and drawing was time spent away from family duties. I loved books, too, which they didn't mind as much. But I had little time to follow my passion, as I was kept busy with chores, schoolwork and family squabbles.

Being the staunch Catholic that my father was, he expected us to go to church every Sunday. My mother wasn't as devout. She didn't go to Sunday mass at all. This was the saving grace for me and my siblings. We would use the excuse that since Mum doesn't have to go, neither do we. The other reason we managed to get out of going to Sunday mass was because we attended Catholic schools, through which we had to attend mass every week anyway.

I attended an all-girls Catholic school, and like a lot of children, I didn't like the structure of church. Every Friday morning, we had to go to mass, and we had to wear a full uniform, including a beret. The nuns and schoolteachers escorted us to church.

On one occasion, I was sent to detention after mass. I'd been standing beside my best friend, and we were singing one of the hymns. All of a sudden, I looked over at my friend because I'd heard her gulp; she then started splattering and spitting. She'd swallowed a fly and was trying to spit it out! I couldn't help myself: I started to laugh. Then both of us were laughing, creating a raucous disruption. One of the nuns saw us laughing. She turned to us, hissing at us to keep quiet, but it was just too funny, and we couldn't stop. The nun came over and hauled us both out of the church and into detention. I really did not enjoy school. I couldn't wait to put the school years behind me and get on with my life.

Another time, I remember the school bell had rung, signalling the end of the day. I was getting ready to walk out of the classroom when one of the nuns called me over. Out of the blue, she asked me to consider becoming a nun! I was shaking at the thought! I think she specifically targeted me because she knew I had a number of sisters. In her opinion, it wouldn't matter if one of us became a nun because there were other siblings to get married, have children and produce grandchildren for my parents.

I was speechless! No way! I thought to myself. I stood there as she proceeded to tell me how much the Catholic schools needed more nuns. Although I knew her intentions were well-meaning, becoming a nun was the furthest thing from my mind. I had dreams of becoming a writer or photographer—or maybe a make-up artist. I'd even pictured myself writing television advertisements. I wanted to be like Darrin from the American sitcom Bewitched. I knew my future lay in something creative. From that moment on, whenever I saw this particular nun, I did everything I could to avoid her.

My father would have been proud of me if I had become a nun, but the life of a nun was not for me. Dad would often remind us of how the nuns in Lebanon had saved him from hardship and gave him an education. When he was a toddler, he lost his father in a tragic accident. Times were very tough in the 1930s. When his father died, Dad, his two sisters and his mother were left without a breadwinner. His mother was unable to care for him. Fortunately, being from a Catholic family, my father was sent to a French boarding school run by nuns. My grandmother believed the nuns would give him a better education than she could. My father stayed at the boarding school until he was old enough to get a job.

Looking back, I guess my siblings and I have been fortunate compared with my father. At least we grew up at home all together—even though we did fight.

Throughout my 20s, my life was fairly stable. It was socially stable in the sense that I had a group of girlfriends with whom I enjoyed going out. We'd go to the movies, to a bar or out for dinner. I didn't particularly enjoy discos or nightclubs, which were a huge part of the scene during the '80s, so on the nights my friends did that, I would stay home. One friend and I were keen to travel overseas, so we saved for almost a year before taking off for Europe for four months. That was the highlight of my early 20s.

When I returned from Europe, I decided it was time to kickstart my writing career. The first step was to enrol at college, study advertising and communications, and learn to write ads and scripts. What surprised me was that I would continually get top marks for my scriptwriting. I was studying at night, which allowed me to work during the day. While I was still studying, I managed to get a job writing marketing brochures for a well-known creative agency. This is where my writing career sprouted. The groundwork was done, and the seed was planted. Later, I would transition from copywriter to journalist and author. I also met my first husband while working at an advertising agency. Life was pretty good for five or so years.

Until my annus horribilis—the year everything changed—the year I turned 30.

Yep, just before I turned 30 I was made redundant from a job I loved, only to discover that I was pregnant! The following week was also when I first learned that my mother had cancer. Nothing changes your life more than losing a loved one, having a child and losing a job. I got the trifecta! These events were very sobering. One of these—alone—can change a life, and I had to go through all three of them at once.

The agency I was working for was going through difficult times, as were many advertising agencies at the time. Eleven people were laid off, and I was one of them. I hadn't expected to be made redundant, and it shocked me. Shortly after I left, I discovered I was pregnant, which eliminated any chance of my finding future work … well, at least for a year or so.

So there I was, pregnant and without a job, only to be hit by the most devastating news of all: that my beloved mother had terminal cancer and had very little time left. There was no time to enjoy the pregnancy; all I could think about was my mother—and the fight that lay ahead for her. Mum fought hard for more than a year, but sadly, the cancer won. My life as I knew it had changed forever. Mum passed away at the age of 51.

In saying this, each of these events has made me a better person. My gorgeous son David was born. From day one, he was a delightful, funny and beautiful little boy, and he gave me so much joy in the midst of the pain of losing my mother. Her death taught me that life is short. She taught me to seize the day and to take every opportunity to live life and achieve my dreams. The loss of my job made me work even harder to become a writer and an author. In retrospect, had I stayed in the advertising industry, I may never have become an author.

It was at that point that I really began questioning my life. Where was I going, and what did I want to achieve? I started listening more to my inner voice and realised that I needed to be more open to really hear what it was telling me. Since that time, my intuitive voice has played a huge role in the decisions I've made—everything from which job to take to where to go on holiday and where I need to be at any given moment. I've had strong feelings and a sense of knowing how certain events would pan out. When I have chosen not to trust this feeling, I've always regretted it.

We've all been in situations in which we've had to make important decisions. Often, your gut instinct tells you to go one way, but your head is pushing you to go another. When you make a decision based on fear or external pressures from other people, the decisions generally come from the head, not from the heart or intuition. We've all fallen into that trap.

It's the same every time: When you have that feeling of knowing that you shouldn't do something but go against your better judgement, you nearly always regret it. For example, you may have chosen to trust someone even though you felt a sense of uneasiness around them, and eventually you find that they betray your trust.

This in-built sense of uneasiness is your very own internal alarm and protection. Any uneasiness you feel around a situation or person is your intuition warning you. You might feel a sensation in your gut, or you may feel highly anxious. I believe intuition is the most powerful and underused tool we have in the human mind. Why? Because intuition acts as your guide and is your internal protection. It takes a lot of courage to listen to your intuition. No one has your best interest at heart more than you do. So listen to your intuition.

During difficult periods, I have turned to my intuition for guidance. Intuition is the one thing I have learned I can count on. It takes time to get used to it and to learn that you can trust yourself and rely on your judgement.

Listening to my inner voice has helped me find the right job, has led me to the right publisher for my books and has provided an enriched life through many experiences. Often, I've taken a leap of faith and trusted my intuition. This book is a testament to that. Throughout the story, I share examples in which intuition has helped me.

I've chosen to make this a personal account of how my intuition led me on a journey of self-discovery followed by a spiritual adventure that took me across the globe. These events are real and have had a profound effect on my life. I found answers to two prophetic dreams. I found love. And most of all, I found peace within myself.

I work as a business and financial journalist. I write with truth, accuracy and integrity. Some of my colleagues will be surprised that I have written a book like this one, particularly coming from my business-reporting background. But what happened to me as a result of listening to my intuition is a story I want to share—to help others who have longed to follow their instincts but are scared.

The purpose of this book is not to be self-indulgent but merely to give other people hope that they can believe in their dreams and listen to their inner voice. Speaking of dreams, my story starts with a very interesting dream that I had in 2011.

All I ask of you, dear reader, is that you keep an open mind.

Thank you.
Emily Chantiri 2013

www.emilychantiri.com.au

Preface

Many of you will remember the cartoon character Casper the Friendly Ghost. Casper is a cute little ghost who would help his friend Wendy the Good Witch whenever she was in strife. When I was very young, I thought everyone had their own Casper guiding them through life. I honestly thought Casper was guiding me because I often received messages when I needed help.

How silly this sounds now, but at six years of age, I didn't know any better. It wasn't until I was about eight that I realised what I had taken to be Casper was really my conscience or intuitive Voice. By then I was old enough to understand that Casper was a cartoon figure and wasn't real. Phew ... what a relief it was to know that no ghosts floated around me.

I can't recall any specific events when Casper appeared; it wasn't like that. It was just that I had a sense of someone being near me and looking after me. As an adult, I guess the closest example would be what people call a guardian angel, even though I'm not sure that's what I'd call it. Many people believe in guardian angels, and they call on their angels to help them through life, so in that sense, it is similar.

I know some people call on their loved ones who have passed away, asking them for help or advice. In my opinion, messages from your guardian angels and deceased loved ones are different from your intuition, because intuition comes from within; it's your voice guiding you as opposed to that of someone else.

I guess that's the role Casper—or should I say my inner voice—played for me. I would call on that inner voice whenever I wasn't sure about what to do. Mind you, I was so young, and the situations I am referring to were mostly about falling out with my friends or my brother, with whom I often fought. I guess I'd sometimes ask for help if there was trouble at school, but as I said, I don't recall the details. My calling on this inner voice was no different from other children who have imaginary friends, except my ghostly friend would later turn into my intuition, otherwise known as my inner voice. It's a gut feeling that I still experience today.

I do remember one situation in which my intuition became a lifesaver. I was 13 years old, and my two youngest sisters were in the bath together. They were toddlers. Mum had stepped away from the bathroom for a few seconds, and I don't know why, but I ran into the bathroom and found one of my sisters lying flat on the bottom of the bath, struggling to get up. She was drowning in the small tub. My other sister was playing alongside her, totally unaware of what was going on. Why did I run in and what made me do it? I can say only that I had a strong gut reaction and felt that something was wrong.

As the years progressed, intuition became my friend, my guidance and my protector. I learned to rely on it more and more. I believe it can be the same for you.

Too often we forget to use intuition, instead we'd rather put that trust in other people, and not in our inner guidance. Intuition is a great confidence builder; the more you use it, the more confidence you'll get from trusting your own judgement.

Intuition is at the heart of this book, and as you read through the pages, I am certain that a few of my experiences will resonate strongly with some of you. I also hope that from reading this book, you will learn to trust your intuition, especially whenever you have tough decisions to make.

Chapter One

Myrtle, Myrtle

"I am the voice of intuition, and to those who are receptive, I speak,"
Meher Baba.

Let me begin this story with a prophetic dream that came to me just before 6.30am on Friday, 18 March, 2011.

I am sitting alone in an old church. I look up, and I see a priest walking towards me. In his hand is a piece of paper. He says, "You must take this message to the people," and then he shows me the piece of paper. I lean over to read the message. Written on the first line are two words:

Stay Myrtle [and something I can't see].

I can't read the rest of the line because the priest's fingers are covering whatever follows Myrtle.

The next couple of lines read:

Stay happy and content.
At the end of 13 days see what comes.

In the dream, I look up at the priest: "Myrtle? What do you mean?" I ask him.

I want to ask him to move his fingers because they are covering crucial words at the end of the first sentence. But I don't, and I feel exasperated. I plead with him: "I can't read the last word after Myrtle!"

At that point, I woke up. *What a strange dream*, I thought. I wondered whether it meant something, albeit something strange and cryptic. Stay Myrtle? Who, or what, was Myrtle? I repeated the words from the dream in my mind. *Myrtle* meant nothing to me, and I had no reference for the word.

I understood that it could be a girl's name, but I had never met anyone by the name of Myrtle, nor was I aware of it being a place or street name. I'd heard of the myrtle plant, yet even that had no special relevance to me.

I was in two minds about whether to get up, but I knew I mustn't get out of bed before writing down the dream's message. I've had prophetic dreams in the past. They feel different from regular dreams because they often have messages in them. I know from past experience that it's best if I immediately write down the message, because if I wait too long and try to remember the dream later, I've often forgotten it. Dreams are easier to remember upon wakening.
*There is more information about dreams below.

I always keep a notepad beside my bed, so that if I get an idea or a thought pops into my mind during the night, I can write it down quick smart; otherwise, I know I will forget it by morning. After I'd written down the dream's message, I was lying there tossing and turning for a while. I couldn't get the word Myrtle out of my head. Over and over I thought about it. What did it mean? Who was Myrtle?

At that point, Myrtle meant nothing to me. Little did I know that the answer was not too far away, through a strange twist of events. Upon waking, I never imagined that the dream would see me travel halfway across the world to unravel its mystery.

With Myrtle on my mind, I got out of bed and went downstairs to my computer. I wasn't ready to let the Myrtle dream completely go away. I felt strongly that there was a specific message in it for me, so I began to search the internet to find the origins of the word Myrtle. Perhaps this would shed some light on the strange message.

After searching online for some time, I found various definitions and origins of the word:

i) An evergreen shrub, myrtle is associated with birth and rebirth in European mythology. The ancient Greeks carried myrtle with them when they colonised new lands to symbolise the beginning of a new life. The Greeks also associated myrtle with Aphrodite, the goddess of love.
ii) Myrtle \m(y)-rt-le, myr-tle\ as a girl's name is pronounced MER-tel. It is of Latin origin. Botanical and nature name based on the evergreen shrub that was sacred to Venus as a symbol of love. First used in the 1850s.
iii) Myrtle is known as the flower of the gods and is associated with the mythological Greek goddess Aphrodite: the goddess of love. In medieval times, myrtle was used as a garland by brides.

iv) When its leaves are crushed and made into oil, it is very fragrant.

v) Dreaming of myrtle means good fortune and a long life.

vi) If you grow a myrtle bush on either side of your door, it will bring love and peace to the household. The Greeks and Romans often drank myrtle tea to keep their love strong.

A further search also suggested that if you dream of myrtle, it means good luck. After scanning the internet for almost half an hour, I concluded that all these meanings were positive and that there was a particularly strong focus on love. In the context of my dream, did this mean Myrtle might stand for love?

I thought further about this. If I were to translate my dream, perhaps it just meant that I must stay loving and contented, and after 13 days, something might happen. Hmm, perhaps I may find love?

The thought of love intrigued me. I'd been single for almost four years, since my divorce in 2007. My marriage had lasted almost 20 years, and the break-up was incredibly difficult—not just for me but also for my children. Now that some years had passed, I felt it was time to start dating again. The thought of meeting someone new and being in love was exciting. Before I could process this thought any further, my teenage son, Mike, came downstairs.

"Mum, why are you up so early, and what are you doing on the computer?" he asked me.

"I need to find some information," I hastily replied.

My response appeared to satisfy his curiosity. Being a typical 14 year old, his interest in mum's affairs was limited. He prodded me no further and began to get ready for school. I headed to the kitchen to prepare Mike's lunch for school. Then I went upstairs to change into my sweats before heading out for my morning walk.

I watched Mike leave for school a little after 7.30am, and shortly after, I stepped out into the sunshine and made my way along the narrow streets to a café. The morning sun was already strong. March is a particularly hot and humid time of year in Sydney. Most mornings before arriving in the office, I'd go out for an early morning walk, grab a coffee and read the papers at a local café.

For the past four and a half years, I'd been working as a business journalist for a leading business magazine. The coffee following my morning walk gave me time to read through the main headlines in the papers. The general pace of working in a large media organisation and meeting deadlines is very intense, with little time to read other than to research stories, so I immensely enjoyed my morning solitude.

As I walked to the café, my dream played over and over in my head. Stay Myrtle [something]... stay contented ... the next 13 days, see what happens. Stay Myrtle ... stay contented ... see what happens. I calculated that 13 days would take me to 31 March or 1 April. What was going to happen? Did the month of April hold some significance other than the fact that it was Easter? After all, in the dream, I was sitting in a church. I was raised as a Catholic—though I have fairly liberal views on religion—but I wondered whether there was some relevance to Easter.

I consider myself to be a spiritual person rather than someone with strong religious beliefs. In my view, religion or spirituality is a personal journey and should not be forced. Each of us is entitled to follow our own religion or beliefs.

When my marriage ended four years earlier, I found myself longing to find the peace and strength to continue with my life. I reached out through my religion and started going back to church. The marriage break-up was hard, particularly as I knew that I had overstayed the marriage and that the love had run out. It was a tough decision for me to be single, and the prospect of raising two children had been daunting, but when the decision came to end the marriage, I felt like a huge weight had lifted off me. Going back to church helped me feel grounded and provided me with a weekly opportunity during which I wouldn't need to fret about my divorce.

I will admit that my first year as a single mother was one of the hardest of my life. I recall telling my friends that I cried a river, just like the song. Now I get exactly what that song means. My tears weren't so much about regret; they were more about ending an experience that had taken up much of my life. I allowed myself one year to grieve the end of the marriage. Once that year was over, I made a pact that I would not waste another day thinking about the past.

Now, though, as I looked to the future some five years later, I felt that my life was looking brighter. In fact, it felt as bright as the sun as I made my way towards the café along the quaint streets of Sydney's Eastern suburbs. These streets are lined with an eclectic mix of homes, from stately mansions to tiny terraces, all reminiscent of a time gone by. Most of the buildings are heritage-listed and were built around the late 1800s and early 1900s. The cafés, restaurants and trendy boutiques add plenty of colour and culture to the area in which I live. I often think about how fortunate I am to reside in this part of Sydney.

As I entered the café and ordered my usual soy cappuccino, I read the papers and quickly drank my coffee just like any other day. But on this day, I was eager to get back home to my computer. I decided that once I got back, I'd send an email to a few friends, recounting the message from my dream. Perhaps the Myrtle dream held some significance to someone I knew. After all, the priest had instructed me to take the message to the people before he'd shown me the piece of paper. Seeing that the message didn't seem to have any significance for me, I thought it may have meaning for someone I knew. I've had other dreams and strong intuition about situations in the past, and sometimes I've felt the need to share those messages with people. But it's been only with a select few.

By nature, I am cautious, and I don't want to appear weird or wacky. If someone has never experienced strong intuition or had a prophetic dream, then it can be hard for them to get their head around the concept. Some people I know have a closed mindset to anything they cannot see or experience for themselves, so I was reticent about emailing many people about my dream. But I knew a few close friends who would understand.

Before I proceed, I want to point out that I do not consider myself a psychic. I prefer to say that I have a highly developed intuitive voice. We all have it. I call it the quiet inner voice of reason, and I talk more about it in the next chapter.

After the dream, my inner voice was very strong and was telling me to research more about the word Myrtle. The word continued playing on my mind as I rushed back home from the café. Back at my computer, I emailed my dream to a few select friends. I decided I would also send some of the meanings that I had uncovered.

It wasn't long before I received a few responses.

My youngest sister Suzie sent this email message:
Hi Em, this is interesting. Did you know that 13 days brings us to Easter, which represents Christ's rebirth and resurrection? Could it mean a new start or something like that for you?

Hmm, yes, I did think about the Easter thing, but I wasn't convinced.

Another friend, Natalie, sent me this response:
Thank you, that's fantastic—it's exactly what I needed to hear. I will switch my cranky pants to loving kindness. I will be in touch at the end of the month to let you know what happens. I will also look for a myrtle plant.

Another of my close friends, Karen, sent the following message,
Wow Em, I got the chills when I read this. I want to rush off and get some of that myrtle. I wonder if it could mean "Say myrtle" as a meditation mantra, rather than "Stay myrtle"? I guess both make sense.

I received a few more responses, but none of them hit home for me. I felt the message was still yet to be revealed.

For the time being, though, I figured if the message didn't mean anything to my friends or family, then I would not dwell on it any longer. Perhaps I was reading too much into the dream, and it was not a prophetic message. That's what my rational mind was telling me.

Yet, as things would turn out, I didn't have to wait long to find the meaning. In a little more than two weeks, the Myrtle message would take on a life of its own that would see me travel to the US in search of answers.

Chapter Two

Intuition

You may be wondering how I know the difference between my inner voice and everyday thoughts. For me, the inner voice is sometimes so loud and clear that it's almost impossible to ignore. On occasion, I've chosen to ignore it, such as the time I felt something was wrong with my car and started to drive it only to discover that I had a flat tyre. I wished I had looked around the outside of the car before I got in—the tyre was flat as a pancake! I drove for a short while and then had to find the nearest petrol station to fill the tyre with air. But the damage was done, and I needed to completely replace the tyre. I still curse myself for not listening to my instincts that day. When it comes to intuition, I think some of us choose to listen to it more than others, but ultimately, we all have access to it.

Intuition is what I call the voice from the heart: It's where all the answers we seek lay—deep within us. It's taken me a while to understand this, but time and time again, whenever I've been trying to make the right decision on an issue, the answer is always there, deep inside. I just had to learn how to tap into it.

Back in 2000, I was writing a book and was searching for a publisher. I wanted to contact a journalist friend, Jennifer, because I knew she had contacts in the book-publishing industry. The problem was that I had lost contact with Jennifer and hadn't seen her for a few years. I knew she lived quite close to me; I just wasn't sure where.

One morning when I was out for an early walk, I had a very strong internal feeling guiding me to a café that I did not usually frequent. I felt a strong pull to go to the café. This is what I mean when I say intuition, or inner voice—it's when you feel so compelled to do something or go somewhere even though your rational mind has no idea why. That day, when I followed the voice, I walked into the café and there was Jennifer—reading the paper!

Stunned, I approached her with a little trepidation. She looked up and was equally surprised to see me. She greeted me and asked me to join her. I sat beside her, and we began chatting away. Our conversation moved towards our jobs and some of our writing assignments. I told her I had an idea for a book and asked her whether she knew anyone in the publishing world. To my delight, Jennifer was very receptive. "Yes," she said. "Try calling my friend Rachel. She's an editor at Random House Australia. I haven't got her phone number on me, but call Random House and ask for Rachel."

Wow! I was speechless. I couldn't thank Jennifer enough for her generosity in passing on this information. I had been hoping to get back in contact with Jennifer, and then my intuition had drawn me to a café I don't usually frequent, and bingo! She is in that very café and gives me the number of a book contact! It all happened as if by magic.

In the back of mind, I was amazed at the chance of something like this happening—just when I'd been thinking that I needed to get a hold of Jennifer. Was this just serendipity? Hmm …

I rushed home and immediately phoned Rachel. Unfortunately, my call went to voicemail. I was tempted to hang up and try again later, then decided against it. This was my chance. I left my phone number and a brief message outlining the idea behind the book. The message I left was a brief run-down of the book club I was in and the women involved. The book I was writing would tell how we came together, how we turned our book club into an investment club, and how we then began trading shares. The members each shared a common bond in wanting to educate ourselves about being financially smart. Our investment club had already become successful: Word had got out that a group of women were investing in the stock market with relative success, and we even had a waiting list for people wanting to join our club.

The club was about each of us learning to become financially independent. And that's how I had the idea to write our story. I believed that women wanted this sort of information, and here was an opportunity to tell the stories in a book of our club and how to do what we had done. Within the hour of my leaving the message, Rachel phoned me back, said she liked the idea and asked me to send over the manuscript. Shaking with excitement, I immediately sent over the manuscript to Random House. I had no idea how long I would have to wait before hearing back.

My gut instinct was very strong. I felt for sure that I would get a contract and have the book published. It just felt so strong: The idea was topical, the meeting with Jennifer was fortuitous and I'd easily gotten the number of a publisher, so I felt sure that everything was lining up for it to happen. I really felt confident about it. Yet on the other hand, I also figured that every writer probably feels that way about his or her book.

Three days after sending my manuscript, I received a call from Rachel. She loved the idea. Although it still needed some work, Random House was going to publish the book. *The Money Club* became a bestseller in Australia when we launched it in 2001. I sometimes wonder whether that book would ever have been released had I chosen not to listen to my intuition that day.

Even some 12 years later, the book is still available. This was one of those moments that I felt so strongly that the book had to be written. My gut instinct said I had to write this story and stay committed right through to the end. Some would call it luck, but I know it was more than that. The powerful inner voice pushed me to go into that café, which in turn led to a publishing deal in less than a week.

Was my dream the voice of intuition? Did other people receive voices as loud and clear as I did, and why aren't we tapping into this more? As my mind wandered back to the myrtle dream, I began to think about the powerful force that is locked deep down in our hearts. I had previous evidence that when my inner voice is really strong, I mustn't ignore it. Even that day when I had no idea I would bump into Jennifer and that it would lead to a book-publishing deal, I just knew I had to follow my instincts. Like I've said, sometimes I have ignored that inner voice, but I'm glad I listened to it that day!

Coming back to the present day, I now find myself with a book on the subject of the inner voice. The topic is very different from that of my other books. I've wanted to write this book for the past five years, but I struggled to bring it together. Part of me questioned whether I'd be taken seriously. I felt that it would take away from my role as a financial journalist. What would my peers think when they heard that I've written a book on intuition and dreams? I've carved out a successful career by being taken seriously, so even though my intuition has led me to great opportunities in the past, I still struggle with completely accepting it. I'm a down-to-earth business journalist, and yet here I am writing a book on a subject that some people would dismiss as kooky or weird.

Interestingly, some of the business people I've interviewed have said they rely on their intuition, which I guess makes me feel more comfortable about writing this. One recent example is a wealthy businessman whose name I am choosing to withhold. This person has done wonderful work within the community and is a notable Australian. I contacted him through his office. After a few email exchanges, he responded by telling me that he felt intuitively keen to go ahead with the interview despite the fact that he rarely gives interviews to the media. I liked his response and said that I was happy that he felt intuitively about the interview. He told me he uses his intuition a lot.

After he agreed to be interviewed, his next email explained that he feels it's important to close the gap between there being intuitive people and "business" types, as deep down he believes we all rely on our intuition—we just might not label it that way. He is not the only successful person I've interviewed who admits to using his or her intuition. I've interviewed numerous successful people who've launched their business ideas based on a strong sense of intuition. They've told me that they just knew they were on the right path.

I began to think of other messages and dreams I'd had over the years. I remembered a message in a dream given to me in the early half of 2009. It was while I was contemplating the idea for this book. At that stage, I had published four books on women and money, and I had no desire to write another book on that subject.

This particular dream message came in the early hours of the morning before I got up. I heard a clear, soft voice whisper in my ear: "Write from the heart, Emily." When I got up, I instantly knew that these words would appear on the cover of my next book (the one you're reading now!), although at that stage, I had no idea what form it would take. I grabbed a large exercise book and wrote the title on it: *Write from the Heart.* Yep, that would be the name of the book I felt I was going to write, and it would be all about the inner voice.

I kept that exercise book beside my bed, waiting for the day when the inspiration would come and the words would write themselves. I had no idea that it would all tie in to my dream about Myrtle, and I definitely had no idea how it would change my entire life.

In a strange twist of fate six months later, I would learn where that soft voice came from, but until then, I kept the book in a small cabinet beside my bed, reaching out to it every now and then, making small notes on the subject of the inner voice, and wondering how it would all turn out. As time moved on, the push to write on the subject of the inner voice became stronger.

Keeping a Dream Journal

People have asked me how they can interpret their dreams. Although I don't keep a specific dream journal, I do have a notepad beside my bed. It's common for writers to have a notepad on them at all times, mainly to jot down ideas. The notepad next to my bed is usually filled with a smattering of work notes and the odd dream. But I do find that if I write down my dream and read over it the next day, I often see some symbolism in the dream that has helped me solve a problem in my life.

If you want to learn about the messages in your dreams, then it's important to write down the dream or the message.

Keep a pen, diary or notepad by your bed. Whenever you have a dream, you must write it down immediately when you wake up. Write down as much detail as possible, including any words or messages you receive. Write down the images, textures, colours, emotions, people and, most important, the words—if you can recall them.

Make sure you write down the time and date of the dream. Most of my powerful dreams have come in the early hours of the morning.

Do not dismiss an idea or message that could later prove to have significant meaning; many famous artists, musicians and inventors had their ideas come to them in a dream.

If you don't intuitively know the answer or the message that the dream is giving you, leave the message for a day or so and then come back to it.

Try a dream-interpretation book. Although I have never used one, it may help you find the answer to a dream, particularly if the dream is a recurring one.

Tony Crisp is a renowned dream expert. If you want to find out more about your dreams and what they mean, visit his website at http://dreamhawk.com. Crisp is also the author of *The Dream Dictionary*.

Chapter Three
Karen and Bali

A few years before my Myrtle dream, I had a strange experience while I was holidaying in Bali. The event shook me so much that even today I get chills when I think about it.

My friend Karen and I have been friends for more than 20 years. During that time, we've shared some wonderful experiences together. Our time in Bali was one of those wonderful times.

Karen is a gifted painter and has had a number of exhibitions in both Australia and New Zealand. I met Karen through my ex-husband when the two of them worked for the same advertising agency. Both are New Zealanders, and they instantly became friends. Karen moved to Sydney in the early '80s and married an Australian. Unfortunately, that marriage ended, but it did produce twin boys. After her divorce, Karen moved back to New Zealand to be nearer to her parents.

In 2008, Karen and I found ourselves divorced single mums, each raising two boys. When Karen came to Sydney for a brief summer holiday in December 2008, we decided to plan a trip together. The plan was to get away to somewhere warm during the coming winter months. We had six months to decide on a destination and book our holiday.

I was particularly keen to get away, as the effects of my divorce had taken their toll on my wellbeing. From the stress of the divorce proceedings, I had lost considerable weight. I needed a break to de-stress, meditate, eat well and regain my health. So when my divorce finally came through in April 2009, a holiday was just what I needed. Bali was the first place that came to my mind.

I'd never previously felt inclined to visit Indonesia, even though Bali is a frequent holiday destination for many Aussies. So when Bali popped into my head, I was initially surprised, particularly as the country had been ravaged by terrorism. In 2002 and 2005, Bali was torn apart by bombings that killed hundreds of innocent locals and tourists.

When I first put the idea of Bali to Karen, she was not in favour of going. She feared more riots or, even worse, more bombings. "What if something happens to us? Our boys still need us," she reasoned. I could hear the anxiety in her voice. I understood her fear and almost relinquished the thought of going, but the pull inside me to go to Bali was very strong; I had to go. Actually, it was my intuition pushing me to go.

Most tourists flock to Bali to visit the beaches and bars and to surf. This wasn't my scene. Instead, I was being pulled towards Ubud, an artists' colony and cultural village in the Balinese mountains. On further investigation, I learned that the streets of Ubud are littered with paintings and artworks all done by the locals. Rice paddies, tropical rainforests and palm trees surround the region. The temperature is much cooler than that on the coast and at the beaches, and I knew I just had to go.

Karen, with her blonde hair and fair skin, is by no means a beach bunny. She warmed to the idea of visiting a retreat in the mountains. The fact that it was an artists' haven appealed to her. We also considered other travel options, such as New Caledonia and Tahiti, but these are generally frequented by honeymooners and couples. Given that we were both recently divorced, that wasn't what we wanted. Bali's other appealing aspects were the Indonesian culture and the food.

We contemplated travelling to an Australian resort, such as Hayman or Hamilton Island but found that these places were just as expensive, if not more so, than flying to Bali. The thought of travelling overseas and experiencing a different culture was a far more attractive option. I longed to get away and, most of all, for both of us to indulge in some Indonesian food!

The gravitational pull towards Bali would not let up, and I couldn't let it go. I strongly felt this was the place we were meant to go. In the end, I convinced Karen. I found some cheap flights and accommodation online, and we flew to Bali for a week in July 2009. When we arrived in Ubud, we discovered we could not have chosen more idyllic accommodation.

The resort had only seven huts on the property, each one structurally designed in keeping with the traditions of Balinese huts. Our hut had a thatched roof with an opening to allow the natural light through. Unfortunately, it also let in a few other insects and animals. On several occasions, we'd find a bird or lizard in our room. One evening, a bird flew into the hut and flapped all around the room. We jumped in fright and spent some time trying to usher it back out into the night air.

Each hut was secluded and surrounded by a magnificent lush tropical garden with palm trees and wildlife. The resort had an infinity pool that perched on the end of a cliff. The pool's water gave the illusion that it flowed down to the valley below. Every morning, I would sit at my favourite spot by the pool and spend time looking across at the rice paddies in the distance. There was also a sea of palm trees that stretched as far as my eyes could see.

During our first few days in Ubud, Karen and I spent much of our time wandering through the main streets, weaving our way in and out of little shops, eating in the tiny cafés and restaurants, and drinking plenty of delicious juices. Watermelon was my favourite, and because the air temperature was so hot, I loved to drink the chilled juices.

Many of the tiny streets were filled with crafts and knick-knacks from local artists. In the centre of town, there was a huge market to which many tourists made their way to find a bargain and haggle on the price of souvenirs, clothing, and other bits and pieces. Karen bought herself a fake designer watch and wallet. Unfortunately, it wasn't long before the watch broke. The wallet didn't fare too well, either. "Cheap things always costs a lot," my mother used to say. She was right, quality and "the real deal" last longer, but we were having so much fun in Bali!

I'm a bit of an anomaly as far as women go, because I dislike shopping, and I'm not keen on markets, either. Karen, on the other hand, likes to shop, but I was relieved to learn that she didn't particularly like markets, so we avoided that scene altogether. The most enjoyable part of the trip for me was lying in the pool and looking across the valley. Here I was miles away from the rest of the world and miles away from work.

On the third day of our trip, one of the most profound events happened to me, and it would significantly impact my life. It occurred while Karen and I were heading back to our hut after our early morning walk. As we walked through the resort's tropical garden, I suddenly stopped in my tracks. Karen was several feet behind me.

I felt a tingling sensation rising through my body. At first, I thought I had walked through a massive spider web, but when I looked closer, there was nothing there. Then I felt a strange buzz of energy covering my whole body. I stood frozen, as what felt like a huge charge of electricity went right through me. The incident lasted for approximately five seconds.

My body began to shiver uncontrollably. The hairs on my arms stood up. I felt as though an unknown force had walked right through my body. I would later learn that, in fact, something *had* walked right through me. If you have ever watched a horror movie in which a ghost walks directly through someone, it felt exactly like that. I was frozen stiff while feeling something vibrating and going right through me. It was incredibly powerful, and it scared me.

Karen who still behind me could see that I was shaking yet frozen at the same time. "What's wrong? What's happening to you?" she cried out. I was frightened. I could barely talk. "I don't know, but something is going right through me," I told her.

"Something going through you?" she asked. "What do you mean?" I could see that she was scared. Then suddenly, it stopped. I looked across at Karen, unsure of what had just happened. Deep inside, I knew something quite out of the ordinary had occurred. I felt hyper-emotional. At that moment, I was trying to explain to Karen that I thought I'd walked into a spider web and was covered by the web, but there was nothing there.

"What spider web? What are you talking about? There's nothing there!" she yelled at me.

"I know, I know," I said. "But something passed through me; I felt it."

"Stop creeping me out," she responded. "You're scaring me!"

We collected our thoughts, and then Karen asked me how I felt. Was I okay? "Yes, I guess I'm okay," I told her. But I was visibly shaken. I was thinking about what had just happened. Was it something to do with this place that we'd chosen as a resort, right here in the most idyllic location in the mountains?

All kinds of strange thoughts were going through my mind, such as wondering whether I had walked on an ancient burial ground. I know it sounds crazy, but I was beginning to wonder where the hell we were. And why had I wanted to come here? I'd never experienced anything like this before. I had come to Bali expecting a normal, relaxing holiday.

As I'd stood frozen to the spot, something that felt like electricity had gone through me. Yet, unlike being electrocuted, I'd felt no pain, and it hadn't made me fall to the ground. It had felt tingly, but that was all.

Karen and I looked around at the track we were on. There were no loose electrical wires, spider webs or anything else that would have sent an electric-like current through me. It wasn't raining, so there was nothing that I could have stood on that would've sent a charge through me. It was just the bare ground beneath me, and there was no one else around us. It was peculiar, to say the least.

After I'd stopped shaking and tingling, I felt extremely sensitive to the environment and especially the sounds around me. It was as though my hearing and senses had all been elevated to another level. It's hard to explain. At the time, I wondered whether anyone else had experienced anything similar.

Shaken and bemused, Karen and I slowly walked back to our hut. I kept turning around, wondering whether something else was about to happen or if a creature was about to jump out. My nerves were frayed, and I was hypersensitive.

Could there be a spirit on the property? When you're all alone with no one around, it's common for your mind to wander. I'd heard that Bali is a spiritual place, and it did cross my mind that we may have been on sacred ground. It was the only thing I could think of as I tried to make sense of it all. I thought more about that idea as we walked back to the hut. I was spooked, and I'm sure Karen felt the same way.

I was still visibly shaken by the time we reached our hut. I took my time walking upstairs into our room. I turned to Karen and said I needed to say a prayer. Not a prayer in the strictest sense—more of a meditative gesture of gratitude. After what had just happened, I really felt that we were somewhere sacred. I thought that if I said a prayer of gratitude, I might feel calmer. And if there was an evil spirit around, I wanted protection—not that I believed there was anything evil.

I didn't feel like talking. I just wanted to digest what had happened.

Karen asked me whether I wanted some water or tea. "Yes, both," I said. "And anything stronger." While Karen made the tea, I said a small prayer and then went outside, sat on the balcony and tried to calm my nerves.

A couple of months before the trip, I'd purchased a deck of oracle cards. I'd seen them in bookstores, and some friends of mine had them, too. While I was in one such bookstore, I'd been drawn to a set of oracle cards by Doreen Virtue* (I talk more about oracle cards later.) The deck was beautifully and ornately decorated. On each card there was a message from a saint or an angel. As I sat on the balcony, I remembered that I had packed the cards, as I'd recently started using them. I would pick a card each day and read the daily message. I'd planned to show them to Karen, and in hindsight, I'm really glad I packed them.

I went to my suitcase and grabbed the cards. They were the first and only deck of oracle cards I've ever purchased. As I mentioned, this particular deck of cards contained messages from the saints, along with a brief description of the work for which the saint was known. There were daily messages from St Bernadette, St Francis, St Joan of Arc and St Michael the Archangel, among others, and I always felt they provided reassuring messages.

Like I've said, I don't consider myself religious, but I was feeling as though I needed some help from above, so I grabbed the cards and stepped outside on the balcony and placed them facedown on the table. Then I went inside to help Karen.

Just when I thought I'd had enough shocks, another strange thing happened that freaked me out and left me speechless and shaking—again!

With two teacups in my hands, I returned to the table where I'd placed the cards facedown. On top of the deck, one of the cards was standing upright! I did a double take and stood looking at the card. I'd placed all the cards face down. But this one card was standing straight up, leaning slightly on a candle holder, which gave it the support to stand. When I saw the upright card, shivers went through me. How did it stand up like that? My voice failed me.

I was trying to scream out to Karen to get her attention, but I was so petrified that nothing came out of my mouth. I was stamping my feet, trying to make noise. Finally, Karen heard the commotion. She ran over to me, where I was pointing to the upright card.

"Look, look ... it's upright! By itself!" I managed to squeeze enough of my voice to let these sentences out. "I didn't do it!" It took every ounce of energy I had to say those words.

Karen also began shake.

The upright card was the guardian angel card, and on it was written "Vision".

Karen's face turned pale, and her deep blue eyes opened wide in shock. "Oh my God! Who did this?" she cried out. My voice was barely audible, as I was still petrified. "I don't know," I replied. "I just put the cards down, came back out with the teacups and saw it. Just like that, standing up!"

We searched outside and around the hut, but there was no one in sight. We were alone. I thought about whether the wind could have blown it upright. But there was no wind. It was hot, sticky and humid. Besides, if it had been windy, it would have blown the other cards away.

Each hut was far away from the others. We had complete privacy, and I had disappeared for only a few seconds to get the cups. It would have taken more than a few seconds for someone to leap up onto our balcony, find that particular card and stand it upright against a candle on top of the deck. Also, we would have heard a noise if someone was on the balcony or even if they had been approaching. We had the doors wide open and no one was around.

All I had done was walk away for a second or two to grab the cups. Now my mind started going off again, as I wondered whether I had brought some kind of spirit entity with me. I was meditating a lot, and I know it might sound crazy, but I wanted answers. *Why was this happening to me?* All I wanted was a normal, relaxing holiday away from the pressures of deadlines and business reporting. I couldn't believe this was happening.

Karen and I sat down at the table. We were both trying to come to terms with what had just occurred. I gingerly leaned over to the deck and grabbed the "Vision" card. I said to Karen that maybe the message was significant. I read the message on the back, hoping it might explain what had just happened.

The message read as follows:

This message is about honouring your vision. It asks you to truly trust the mental images that you've been receiving, as they're answers to your prayers. Your prophetic visions will bring blessings to you and your loved ones. You know that they are heaven-inspired because of their loving nature. Only follow the message that asks you to act on behalf of God's love.

The message gave me some reassurance, but deep in my heart I knew this strange experience was about to change the course of my life. How it would change and what was going to happen, I had no idea. Was this the reason I'd felt intuitively pushed to go to Bali?

For the remainder of our time in Ubud, things went relatively smoothly; though we did decide to sleep with the lights on! In the back of my mind, I decided that once I was back home in Sydney, I would try to find out whether anyone else had experienced anything similar.

How to Use Oracle Cards

Oracle cards generally come in a deck similar to regular playing cards. Each card offers a positive message or insight. Unlike tarot cards, which require you to learn how to read and place them, oracle cards are much easier. I don't use tarot cards. I prefer the gentler messages of oracle cards.

These cards come in all shapes and sizes and cover a range of subjects. The queen of oracle cards is Doreen Virtue is an American author and spiritual doctor of psychology. She also has a doctorate in counseling psychology. Virtue put these positive cards on the map and has written many decks that are all very popular.

Reading oracle cards is simple. All you do is shuffle the deck and draw out a card. According to Doreen Virtue, it doesn't matter from which end of the deck you pull the card or cards; the answer will be what you need to know. You can have a question in your mind or simply pull a card and read what it says. The great thing about oracle cards is that they are always positive and uplifting.

Most bookstores and many gift shops sell these types of cards, and they're also available online. There are thousands of different decks. The best one for you will be one that you feel resonates the strongest.

Chapter Four

Vera

Juggling a career and children as a single parent is tough. Aside from the very strange event at the Bali resort, my time I spent in Ubud was wonderfully rejuvenating. I did get time to rest and sit by the pool. The warm weather was exactly what I needed too. I came home with incredible clarity. The incident in Ubud, as strange as it was, appeared to release a block within me, because upon my return, I noticed how my intuitive voice had become much stronger.

In wanting to understand how intuition works, I began to use it more often in my daily life. The more I used it, the more answers I got. I figured that if you practice learning something, you're going to get better at it. And that's what I did with my intuition. After Bali, something in me had changed. I was still more sensitive to my environment, to noise, to food and to people. It was strange but comforting.

Not long after my return from Bali, I decided that I needed to further investigate whether anyone had ever had a "ghostly" experience similar to mine. My first port of call was a New Age bookstore in the city; I hoped I would find something written about paranormal experiences. If I thought that hat had happened in Bali was strange, that was only the start! More and more unusual things began to unfold through my investigation, including one surrounding my visit to the New Age bookstore. That day would eventually lead me to a woman called Vera.

The way that connection came about would have to rate as one of the most bizarre experiences I have ever had.

That day, during my lunchbreak, I went to the bookstore—a 20-minute walk from my office. I didn't have much time, but a work meeting got cancelled, giving me a little more time than usual. I walked briskly, weaving my way around the lunchtime crowds. Other than a couple of customers and retail assistants, the store was empty. I walked past the counter and began searching through the rows of books, looking to find something about paranormal experiences. I stopped at one shelf and grabbed a few books.

I had been in the store for only about five minutes when a woman came over to me. She had short, light-brown hair; was dressed in smart, casual clothes; and looked to be in her early 40s. I had taken a seat and was skimming through the pages of one of the books. I looked up at the woman; she had two young boys, aged about nine and seven, with her.

She looked at me and then, out of the blue, said, "Do you believe in angels?"

A little surprised by the question, I looked away from the book in my hand, and turned my attention to her and her boys. "Huh? Sorry, what did you say?" I asked.

She repeated her question: "Do you believe in angels?"

"Angels? Well, I guess so, but I've never seen an angel."

"I believe in angels and so do my sons," she replied.

"Oh, really ... wow, that's okay ... er, I mean, good," I said. I was unsure about how to respond to this statement about her boys believing in angels, because I knew my sons didn't.

"Your sons ... they believe in them, too?" I asked, looking over at her boys. "I have two boys, and to tell you the truth, they don't believe in angels or anything like that." It was a strange conversation to be having.

The woman proceeded to tell me that she and her sons had just attended a charity lunch to raise money for sick children. I nodded and listened as she continued. "My little girl has been seriously ill," she told me. "My sons and I have seen angels around her bed."

I was taken aback by her story and her openness to share it with a stranger. Now that I was opening up more to my intuition, was this how my life would be? People would randomly come up to me and start talking about angels? I thought it was a bit odd, and again, I wasn't sure how to respond to her comment about seeing angels at her daughter's bed. I told her I was very sorry to hear about her daughter. "She's doing okay," she responded.

I nodded as she said this and looked back at the book in my hand. Then I told her I had come to the bookstore to find some information on an unusual incident that had happened. But before I could even begin telling my story; she interrupted me and asked me whether I had been to a psychic. I thought to myself, *What does seeing a psychic have to do with anything?* I hadn't even told her my story. The sceptic in me was on high alert. "No, I don't visit psychics," I told her.

I explained to her that I was sceptical of psychics' abilities and wondered whether some of them prey on people's vulnerability. However, I also told her that I do believe some people have an ability to read into the future but that I believed they were few and far between.

The woman then said she knew of a lady who was very good and that I must see her. Once again, I repeated that I had no desire to visit a psychic and that I don't really trust them. The woman ignored me and urged me to give the psychic a call. She pulled a small diary out of her handbag and tore out a piece of paper. I watched her as she wrote down the name Vera, which I presumed was the psychic she was talking about, followed by a phone number. "Please call her," she pleaded, then gave me the piece of paper and walked away.

The brief encounter left me stunned. Who was this woman, and why on earth would she ask me whether I believed in angels? And why would she insist that I see a psychic? Was I asking for trouble coming to a bookstore like this? I had come here searching for information about my experience in Bali, and now I found myself having yet another strange experience. The plot just seemed to get thicker by the day. Deep down, though, I knew I'd had such a strong feeling that I needed to come to the bookstore. My intuition had led me here, so maybe there was something in the message from this stranger.

A few seconds passed before I realised I wanted those questions answered, but no sooner had I stood up to find the woman than I noticed she was nowhere to be seen. She had vanished completely—she and her two boys. I looked around the bookstore, and in a matter of seconds, the three of them had disappeared. There was no trace of them, except for the piece of paper with Vera's number on it.

I had the paper she had given me in my hand. I decided to hold onto it, although I was not quite sure of what I would do. For the next few days, I thought about the woman in the bookstore and her insistence that I go to see Vera the psychic. When I thought about the woman in the bookstore, I was sure she looked like an average mother with two young boys. She didn't come across as a New Age wacko. She hadn't tried to sell me something, and she was genuine in the way she talked to me about her daughter and the angels.

I spent a lot of time thinking about that day and how I'd had such a strong feeling inside driving me to visit the bookstore. I knew it was my intuition that had guided me there. Maybe it wasn't so much about finding a book with answers but more about connecting with this woman. Perhaps her psychic friend had the answer to what had happened to me in Bali.

After a lot of deliberating, I decided to call Vera the following week. I would call her on Thursday, a day when I was not in the office. When Thursday arrived, I was nervous about making the call. The logical side of my brain was telling me to not waste my time. This is nuts. Yet my intuitive side was telling me to go for it: Pick up the phone and give her a call. I have to admit, curiosity got the better of me and, I thought, if all else fails, what did I have to lose by making one phone call?

The tussle between my head and my heart continued. My head was saying, "No! Only unstable people see psychics. Why do you need to see one?" But my heart was saying, "Just do it. What have you got to lose? What could go wrong with making a simple phone call. I had been drawn to the bookstore for a reason and perhaps Vera might be able to help me.

After a lot of thought, I thankfully chose to listen to my heart. Later that day, when I found the courage to call Vera, I was surprised to hear a soft, gentle voice at the other end of the line. She gave me a welcome greeting and, instinctively, I felt reassured. From the sound of her voice, I guessed her age to be around 60 or 70. Her first words to me were: "Good afternoon, and how are you today?"

"I'm fine, thank you," I responded. So far, so good. With much apprehension on my part, I was about to begin explaining the strange set of circumstances that surrounded my receiving her number. But before I could even begin the story, she cut me off, saying, "You're a writer! And you've written books!"

I was stunned and shocked by her statement! I dropped the phone, which fell to the floor. How could she know I was a writer? I had hardly said a word other than hello. I hadn't yet uttered a word about myself, nor about the woman in the bookstore. I hadn't even had the chance to tell Vera how I got her number. I remember pinching myself to make sure that I was awake and that this was really happening. I stood shaking for a few seconds before I could pick up the phone. I was speechless. I could hear Vera saying, "Hello ... Are you there? Hello? Hello?"

"Yes," I said in a whisper. I was not sure what to say next. Before another second passed, she began to tell me I was going to write another book. "You will write a book that will help many people," she said. "People are waiting for something like this. They need this book." She continued to tell me that although I had written books in the past, this one would be what people were searching for. She said I would write a book about life. What did she mean, I wondered?

"Life?" I inquired.

"Yes, write about life, your life," she said. "People need this information, and you will write it in 2012. So it can be ready," she said. There was so much going around in my head. *Who was this woman? How could she know I was a writer? She didn't even know my name. Write about my life? I didn't understand why anyone would be interested in my life. And why 2012?* That was still three years away. I was in a state of shock and confusion.

She asked me my name, and then slowly, I began to tell her that I was calling because I'd had a strange experience in Bali. I asked whether she could help me understand what had happened to me in Ubud. Vera told me that she'd heard of similar things happening to other people. She went on to explain that I had moved into another dimension. I thought to myself, *What is she talking about? Another dimension?* I listened as she explained further. "You were so relaxed that you moved into another dimension, and that's when the vibration went through you."

I was finding this all very hard to process. Yes, I had been significantly relaxed while I was in Bali. I had been using meditation to help me. I have by no means perfected meditation, as my mind still wanders, but for the past couple of years, I've been practicing regularly to help relax my mind, even if it is for only 10 minutes at a time. I was gathering my thoughts as Vera explained what had happened to me. Thinking back to Ubud, I'd spent most of the early morning hours down by the pool. More often than not, I was alone, meditating, surrounded only by the tranquillity of the resort's tropical garden and beauty. I had certainly been very calm.

Vera proceeded to tell me that this happened to me because I had been very relaxed and that my chakras, which are energy points in the body must have opened up (more on chakras and their meanings below). To her mind, I had become supersensitive and was probably going through a *kundalini*, or change. *A kundalini? What the hell is that?* I thought to myself. It meant nothing to me.
"Your chakras have opened up," she repeated.

What was she talking about? I've never fully understood what chakras are, and it's only in more recent times that I've come to understand a little more about them and the fact that they are energy points in the body. Vera told me that my third eye had opened up, and then she added, "Your dreams are going to tell you a lot." She reiterated her prophecy regarding the book I would write in 2012. "People are seeking this information, and they're ready for a book like this one," she told me. At that moment, I recalled the notebook I had beside my bed with the words *Write from the Heart* written on the cover. I told Vera that I was working on an idea but that it was still not coming to me clearly.

"Write about your life," she repeated. Her response was very confident. I couldn't understand what she meant about writing about my life. What could I share about my life? Finally, she said that I would travel a lot in the next five years—to America, New Zealand and England. As it turned out, the following year, I *did* travel to New Zealand, which wasn't a surprise because my good friend Karen lives there. But a little more than a year after meeting Vera, my myrtle dream did lead me to the US, three times within a 12-month period. The last time I'd been to the US was 10 years earlier, so when Vera told me this, I couldn't see how any of it would happen. I tried to take in everything she was telling me, but I was still not certain about any of it.

As the phone call came to an end, I realised we'd been speaking for almost an hour. I thanked Vera and asked her why she'd given me all this information. Did she want money? She said she didn't want any remuneration and that she just felt right speaking to me. Before I hung up, I told her I would like to visit her some day—to her personally. She graciously invited me to call her anytime.

In the weeks that followed, my thoughts would take me back to that conversation with Vera. I recalled the strong voice that pulled me to go to the bookstore, which had led to the chance meeting with the woman with the two young boys who gave me Vera's number. One thing was for sure: Vera *did* help shed some light on the Bali incident. I no longer felt the need to search for more answers.

Moving through other dimensions and opening my chakras were things I really didn't fully understand. Yet I felt better knowing there was an explanation, even if it was strange to me. If it meant that my ability to tap into my inner voice was strengthened, then I would accept Vera's explanation.

I accepted that my chakras and third eye were now more open and stronger. I would just accept it all and let the whole thing go. Since that time, I have shared my story with numerous people, and no one has been able to offer any other explanation. This is why I chose to accept what Vera told me, and I will continue to do so until such time as someone can offer another explanation.

Six months after our initial phone conversation, I was still thinking about the impact Vera and the woman in the bookstore had had on me, so I made time to visit Vera. I wanted to keep my promise to thank her in person. During that visit, I would learn something that would stay with me for the rest of my life.

Before arriving at Vera's place, I had no idea what was about to occur. I thought I was on my way to meet a nice lady who had helped me. But things were about to become even more interesting.

The drive to Vera's home was an hour away from where I lived. Vera lived in a typical weatherboard cottage in a suburban street filled with similar houses and much like any other suburban town in Australia. As I had predicted, Vera looked to be in her late 60s and had a lovely, grandmother-like appearance. She was warm, and there was something very comforting about her. She spoke with enthusiasm and had a real spark in her eyes.

When I arrived, she welcomed me with open arms. I was really happy to finally meet her. Before our meeting, we'd talked a number of times on the phone, so when we came face to face, I felt as though I was reconnecting with an old friend. I walked into her house, which was cosy and comfortable. Photos of her children and grandchildren adorned the walls and mantles. Vera had made tea and banana cake and offered me some while I made myself comfortable. She talked about her past, her family and her daughters. She told me she'd been living on her own since she'd divorced her husband some 20 years earlier.

After a few minutes, Vera offered to give me a psychic reading. I decided to go along with the idea and to see what she had to say. I trusted her because we'd spoken a few times, so it didn't feel like I was visiting a psychic. (I still held a healthy level of scepticism.)

Vera led me to a small, comfortable room with a window that looked out to her backyard. The yard was well-kept, with plenty of lawn, an old chicken coop and a few trees. From the window, I could see a small wooden verandah that led from the back door. The room we were in was light and clean, with a couple of soft lounge chairs. Vera asked me to sit down and sat opposite me. She closed her eyes for a few minutes and then proceeded to give me a reading. She didn't use tarot cards or anything like that; she just seemed to be tapping into her inner voice. During the reading, Vera again talked about the book I would write and about my work as a journalist. She also talked about my mother. As she was talking, I noticed that she seemed to be looking over my shoulder, as if she was listening to someone behind me.

Then, completely out of the blue, she said that my mother would help me write the book. Vera brought her gaze to my eyes and said, "She is telling me to tell you to write from the heart." I gasped in shock! I was speechless, and my eyes filled with tears. Up to that point, I must have still had some doubts about her psychic ability, but after she said those words, I no longer doubted that she could tap into something far deeper than I understood. It was all the validation I needed.

"Write from the heart" was exactly the message that had come through in my dream almost a year earlier. Could the voice that I'd heard in the early hours of the morning been my mother, encouraging me to write from the heart? Those were the words I'd written on the notebook in which I had yet to write. I knew—there and then—that I was going to write this book. I was deeply touched by the message that came through Vera from my mother, and although I still find it hard to believe, I knew that the events that had led me to her were too far-fetched to be coincidence. This was still two and half years before my Myrtle dream, but all paths were leading to me write a book about intuition.

To this day, Vera and I remain good friends, and we regularly keep in touch. When I left her that day, I felt uplifted and happy. I knew I had a job to fulfil, even though I was still somewhat unsure about how it would come to fruition. Meeting Vera has helped me believe that some people truly do have a psychic gift and that they can see into the future.

But I must admit, the sceptic in me remains wary. I keep a much more open mind than I used to, but I still believe we are all human and that sometimes the information psychics offer isn't always accurate. People like Vera who have this gift are few and far between. While I trust Vera, she is human after all, and humans make mistakes.

Understanding Chakras

When Vera raised the issue of my chakras opening up, I had no idea to what she was referring. So I investigated their meaning. I discovered that the origin of chakras is found in ancient tantric and yogic traditions in both Hinduism and Buddhism.

Simply put, chakras are energy points within the body. There are seven main chakras, and each has a purpose. These vital points in the body correspond to major physical plexuses of arteries, veins and nerves. When chakras are blocked, it can lead to illness, so chakras must remain free to keep the energy flowing. Regular meditation can help open the chakras. When your chakras are open, it's common to experience a heightened sense of intuition due to the free flow of energy.

The 7 chakras and what they represent:

1. Root Chakra – Foundation for feeling grounded
Located at the base of the spine in the tailbone area
2. Sacral Chakra – Connection to accept others and new experiences
Located at the lower spine in the reproductive area
3. Solar Plexus Chakra – Control over our lives
Located in the upper abdomen and stomach area
4. Heart Chakra – Ability to love
Located in the centre of the chest
5. Throat Chakra – Communication
Located at the throat
6. Third Eye Chakra – Focus on the bigger picture and intuition
Located between the eyes
7. Crown Chakra – Connection to our spirituality
Located at the top of the head

The chakras make up a complex energy system, and many books

and websites can tell you more. Caroline Myss is an American best selling author who has written on this subject. She has some great information that's easy to understand. Visit her website at http://www.myss.com/library/chakras/

Chapter Five

A Hawaiian Storm Before the Dream

In March 2011, a week or so before I had the Myrtle dream, my sons and I spent a week in Hawaii. My time in Hawaii reminded me of my trip to Bali. When I'm on holiday, I'm more relaxed, and the more relaxed I am, the stronger the messages I receive. My Myrtle dream came shortly after a relaxing trip to the US.

The holiday was a family get-together for my sister Rita's birthday. Rita chose Hawaii to celebrate the event. Rita's husband Matt and her daughter Lynn were also there. And another sister, Nadine; her husband, Steve; and their three-year-old son John also came.

The idea was to have a joint sibling holiday, and my sons David and Mike were looking forward to the trip. We agreed that Hawaii would be an ideal destination for us all, as we could engage in a lot of activities together, such as going to Waikiki Beach, sunbathing and swimming.

Although her actual birthday is 14 March, we chose to celebrate it on 11 March because the boys and I were leaving for Sydney on 12 March; the 11th was the last night we would all be together in Hawaii. We were all looking forward to Rita's birthday dinner at the Hard Rock Café in Waikiki.

David and Mike were particularly excited about visiting the infamous restaurant. As soon as we entered, the boys were awestruck by the amount of music memorabilia covering every inch of the place. Mike took great interest in the names of the guitarists whose instruments lined the walls. He'd been learning to play the guitar for the past three years.

The celebration began without a hitch, and the kids got stuck into their meals. There were plenty of burgers, chips and tall glasses filled with fizzy drinks for the kids.

Shortly after 10.00pm, Rita's mobile phone pinged. We were in the middle of singing "Happy Birthday" when a text came through on her phone. It was from our other sister, Noelle, who was home in Australia. The message read: "Is everyone okay?" Huh? We had no idea in what context she had sent the message. Then Matt and Steve both received texts. One by one, we all received messages on our phones. In the midst of all the phones going off, someone mentioned the word *tsunami*. As more messages came through, we learned of an imminent tsunami heading towards the Hawaiian coastline. I looked around the restaurant. Clearly, we were not the only ones seemingly oblivious to the news. Other diners were still sitting and continuing to eat.

While we were trying to make sense of the news, we called over a waiter and asked whether he'd heard of any warnings regarding an imminent tsunami coming towards the island. He was unaware of any tsunami. A couple more minutes passed before the news had well and truly spread and we could see some commotion among the other diners. Suddenly, the waiters ran to us and to all the other diners and said that we had to leave the restaurant immediately. The information was correct: A tsunami was on its way. The staff urged us to get back to our hotels as quickly as possible.

We discovered that a huge tsunami had just hit the Japanese coast and was heading towards Hawaii, the Philippines, Indonesia, Chile and the west coast of the US. Warnings were being issued and people were told to brace for the massive tsunami that was due to hit the coasts of these countries.

As more information came through, we heard that the tsunami was the result of one of the strongest earthquakes on record to strike the region. The 8.9-magnitude tremor shook buildings across Tokyo and unleashed a seven-metre-high tsunami. We immediately left the restaurant and headed back to our hotel. The Ohana Waikiki East hotel was only two streets back from Waikiki Beach, and we hurried back along Honolulu's central shopping strip, Ala Moana Boulevard. Usually, this main drag would be full of tourists, street performers, musicians and hawkers creating a busy hive of activity both day and night. But on this night, the crowds had evacuated. In the background, the sound of police sirens screamed out.

When we reached the hotel, a number of guests were queuing at the front desk. The hotel staff informed us that we were to move to the top level of the hotel and stay indoors. Any guests who were in the lower rooms were moved into rooms on higher levels. I wondered how the hotel was going to cater to all its occupants. How were we all going to fit? Later that night, I saw some guests camped in the corridors.

On the streets, police cars continued to drive slowly, sirens going. A police officer's voice came through a loudspeaker, urging everyone to evacuate the streets. No one was to leave the hotel, and no one was to venture to Waikiki Beach. All beach access was closed. All the guests were moved to floors six and above. The idea was that the higher off the ground you were, the safer you would be if a tsunami hit.

The boys and I had rooms on one of the lower floors. My sister Nadine was on the 16th floor, so we moved in with her, along with Rita, Matt and Lynn. There we were, the nine of us huddled together in one hotel room. We were scared, although we were trying to put on a brave face for the sake of the children. I wanted to stay calm, because if I began to panic, it would make things worse for the kids, who were visibly frightened. It was well past midnight before my sisters could put the two youngest ones to sleep. The rest of us sat by the TV and watched the news for any updates and warnings.

Every hour, the tsunami warning siren went off. In the first hour, the roads were gridlocked as cars escaped from lower-lying areas and headed for higher ground. Within a short time, the streets were eerily quiet, with only the police cars patrolling the streets. Every now and then, we'd hear the voice of a police officer echo through a loudspeaker urging everyone to evacuate or move to higher ground.

Steve and my son David stood guard on the balcony, relaying information about what they could see. At one stage, we heard the sound of glass smashing down below. Can you believe it was looters taking advantage of the situation and raiding the convenience stores whose owners had fled?

My sisters were worried about their children, particularly as they were only three and four years old. "If a tsunami *did* hit, they wouldn't survive if they were to be swept up," Nadine said, clearly distraught. We were all thinking about the tsunami that had hit the Indonesian coast in 2004, tragically killing hundreds of thousands of people. It was hard not to think the worst, though strangely enough, I remained quite calm.

Images of the waves hitting the coast of Japan continued to be splashed across the TV screen. It was frightening. My sons were becoming increasingly anxious. This was not how we'd planned for our trip to end. If Hawaii was going to be hit by the tsunami, it was due to happen around seven hours after it had lashed the Japanese shoreline. This meant that we would get an indication of the severity of the storm by 4.00am.

We watched the news right through the night. Eventually, at approximately 4.00am, we received the news that the Hawaiian coast had been spared from any major damage. The tsunami waves had hit the Hawaiian coast, but the impact was small and the coast was clear—literally! In the midst of all the madness, I remained calm, much to the annoyance of the rest of the family. It's not that I didn't believe in the severity of the situation; it was more about how I chose to handle it. I silently prayed that we would survive, and I prayed for the lost lives of the people in Japan who had no hope or warning. I didn't feel the need to become overly worried. It was as though my intuition told me not to worry, that everything would be all right.

The following morning, the boys and I flew home; the only indication of the night before was that all flights in and out of the airport were delayed by several hours. The tsunami incident was a reminder of how life can be taken away in an instant and how important it is to spend time with family. The boys and I were fortunate to have had a holiday together. We learned that the tragedy had claimed the lives of 19,000 people.

The day after we arrived home safe and sound, the boys returned to school, and I went back to work. After the tsunami ordeal, I welcomed being back in the office, even though it meant going back to the grind of churning out articles with relentless, tight deadlines.

Upon my return, I still had a sense of relaxation from my holiday. Despite the tsunami, I had enjoyed our family trip and wanted the holiday feeling to last. Five days after returning home, I had my Myrtle dream. Because I was still relaxed from the trip, my thoughts were clear, which meant I could tap deep into my dreams. I had the same sense of ease that I'd experienced when I was in Bali before the strange incidents. I was very relaxed, and that had opened my chakras. For me, it seems the more relaxed I am, the more messages I receive. I really don't know whether this is the case—it's just a theory—but regardless, the relaxed feeling from my holiday was still on my mind when I had the dream that changed my life.

Chapter Six

Robert

While holidaying in Hawaii, my sister Nadine and I had had several conversations on the subject of dating. Our discussions primarily centred on whether I would be interested in being in a relationship again. I'd made it quite clear to Nadine that I was content being single.

In the previous two years, I'd tried online dating, but nothing serious had eventuated. Like a lot of people, I found internet dating to be hit-or-miss. I wasn't fond of it and had joined the dating scene only after much persuasion from two girlfriends who convinced me it was worth trying. I'd been on and off one particular dating site. I told Nadine that I had recently put my profile back online, but in the past three months, I'd had only one coffee date.

When I had some spare time or when I was bored, I would reluctantly check the dating site. But I found myself doing this less and less. I was seriously contemplating removing my profile, because I no longer felt interested in dating. I was content and happy with life. I questioned whether I really needed to be in a relationship.

For the most part, I enjoyed my job as a business journalist. I was in the process of relaunching a book I'd written in 2005 called the *Savvy Girl's Money Book*. The book had done well and, the second edition of the book was due to be released in January 2012. Socially, my life was good. I had a tight group of friends with whom I'd regularly go out to the theatre, movies or dinner. And, more important, my sons were getting older, which meant I could take trips away and follow another love: travel writing. I believed I had reached a point in my life where I was genuinely happy.

After chatting with Nadine, I decided that when I got back from Hawaii, I would remove my profile and give up online dating. I had no idea at the time that the decision to remove my profile would change my life in yet another unexpected way. Two weeks passed before I found the time to cancel my dating membership. I logged on to my account and was going through the process of removing my profile when I noticed a photo of a man appeared on the page. If you have ever been on a dating site, you'll know that photos of potential prospects are continuously splashed across the screen. This particular candidate grabbed my attention.

It's hard to recall, but on seeing the photo, I can say only that the man looked pleasant enough. He didn't seem to be anything special, and he didn't look especially attractive, but something pulled me to take a closer look and read through his profile, which was well written and straight to the point. He was direct in his approach and said he was originally from America and had been in Australia for 15 years. I can remember thinking that Americans can be overly confident. But as I read further, he spoke of his love for his children and said that spirituality was important to him. I was intrigued by his profile and decided to send him a message.

To this day, I'm unsure why I sent that message, because it went against my very wish to get off the site, but there I was doing the exact opposite and messaging someone! I had no idea whether he would be interested in me, but I recall thinking that I would give online dating one last try and if nothing eventuated, that would be it. I'd be finished with it for good.

I sent the email, introducing myself and telling him that I liked what he'd written. My email was brief and to the point. The next day, I received an email back. He said his name was Robert and told me he'd been on the site for a year or so. I responded by telling him that I had been about to remove myself from the site when I noticed his profile, which I thought was well written and thorough. He thanked me and said that my profile had little information on it (to quote his words: It was "very spartan!") He was right. I'd written very little about myself. My profile was short, and my photo was hidden. Robert emailed to say he'd been on a few dates but that none of them had led to anything serious.

Over the next week, we exchanged more emails, without any suggestion of the two of us meeting in person. Well, certainly not from him anyway. I decided to be bold and ask him whether we could exchange phone numbers and talk on the phone, rather than correspond through the cumbersome email exchanges on the dating site. To my surprise and disappointment, he was not interested in exchanging phone numbers, let alone meeting in person. *Gosh*, I thought to myself. *Well, that's it for me. He doesn't even want to meet. What a waste of time—all that to-ing and fro-ing with emails for nothing.*

I decided I was done with online dating. I'd given it my last shot, and I was now going to remove my profile. I emailed Robert, relayed my original intention to get off the site, and wished him luck in his pursuits. My intention to remove myself from the site must have made him think twice, because shortly after sending my email, I received one back saying that he would like to meet after all. I was perplexed by the sudden turnaround. Should I go, or should I ignore him? Given that he hadn't wanted to meet in the first place, he could be a loser, or he could just be indecisive. Again, I was in a battle with my rational head saying no and my heart saying I should take a chance.

Once again, intuition won out. Something inside me had propelled me to contact Robert in the first place. After more thought, I decided that yes, I would meet him. I really had enjoyed our email exchanges, and my gut was telling me to give him a chance, even though my head was saying all kinds of other things! We set the date for the coming Sunday night. We arranged to meet at a popular bar on Sydney's trendy Oxford Street, not far from where I lived. The next few days passed without any further news, so I felt fairly confident that Robert wouldn't change his mind.

Past experience had taught me that online dating is very much a numbers game. You have to go through a few dates before you find the right one, or, as some would say, you have to kiss a few frogs before you meet your prince! I found that most first dates would last about an hour, although I'd had one that lasted a torturous 15 minutes. In my experience, a great date would last around three hours. At the time of meeting Robert, I'd had only two of those.

When Sunday came around, I spent much of the day cleaning and washing clothes in preparation for the week ahead. My son Mike was home, so I explained to him that I was meeting a friend but that I would be out for only an hour or so. I told him that if he needed anything, I wasn't going to be too far away. As I was getting ready to meet my new date, I wondered whether it was going to last just 15 minutes or if I would strike it lucky a third time and have another three-hour date. I threw on a pair of black jeans and a casual T-shirt with a pair of black high-heel sandals. I kept my dark, shoulder-length hair free rather than tying it back in a ponytail. I kept my make-up to a minimum, applying just enough to give me some colour.

On my way out, I grabbed a small shoulder bag and went to meet Robert at the bar as per our arrangement. The bar had recently opened and had received rave reviews. When I arrived, I took a look inside and could see that it was busier than I'd expected. Within a couple of minutes, a tall, thin man with short dark hair walked towards me. I watched him slowly approach. "Hello," said Robert. His American accent was a giveaway. I returned his hello and was pleasantly surprised by how attractive he was. I actually did a double take. The photo on his profile played no part in showing off his strong, handsome features."

Well, I thought to myself, *so far, so good; he's on time and good-looking.*

I silently wished I'd made more of an effort with my appearance! We exchanged a few awkward greetings and walked into the bar. Unfortunately, as I'd suspected, the bar was overcrowded, and there was no way we could get in. I suggested trying another pub just down the road. We walked for another five minutes, but even the second pub was full, with patrons spilling out onto the pavement.

With so many people around on a Sunday night, I wondered whether there was a special event. I suggested another bar further up the road. We walked for another five minutes but again the bar was crowded and really noisy. First dates are all about getting to know someone, so you cannot have a first date in a noisy bar. I asked someone in the crowd what was going on. An annual racing carnival had taken place earlier in the day. The race crowd had decided Oxford Street was the place to be, so they'd all hit the pubs and bars. By now, 20 minutes had passed, and Robert seemed to be getting impatient. This wasn't going well, but I couldn't blame him. So far, all we'd done was weave in and out of the intoxicated race crowd and bars.

Thankfully, I remembered one more place that was a little off the main road, a lovely old hotel away from the crowds and noise of busy Oxford Street. I told Robert it was another 10-minute walk; he didn't seem too happy, but he agreed, so we set off. As we approached the hotel, I could see from a distance that seats were available at the outdoor tables. The hotel was a tastefully decorated, grand old building. Some patrons were having dinner and were fortunately far more subdued than the Oxford Street crowds.

Finally, after a half-hour of walking, we were able to sit down and talk. I was so relieved that we'd found a nice quiet place. We pulled up a couple of chairs and sat outside. The evening was cool, and the night sky was clear enough to see the stars. Up to this point, we'd said very little between us. I apologised profusely to Robert for the run-around in finding a place. A small part of me was again beginning to think twice about the whole dating scene. I thought that if this date did not go well, maybe it was an omen telling me I shouldn't date. If this turned out to be the case, I was definitely taking a break from dating.

While I was having these thoughts, Robert looked around the hotel and its surroundings. I gathered he must have approved of the place, because his demeanour changed once we sat down. The hotel was elegant and well-maintained. He nodded to himself as he took in the surroundings. After a minute or so, a waiter came over to us, and we ordered a couple of glasses of wine. I soon learned from Robert that he had arrived in Sydney from the US 16 years earlier. He'd moved here after meeting his Australian ex-wife in India. They'd been married for 10 years and had a son and daughter.

As we enjoyed our wine, we spoke about our backgrounds and the dating scene. We discussed the things we liked and disliked, and we talked about our taste in music, food and spirituality. I told him I'd been brought up Catholic but that I now have liberal views about religion. He didn't say too much on that subject other than that his spirituality was an important part of his life. We talked about our careers: Robert had gained a teaching degree at a US university, but for most of his career he'd been working in the technology industry. I talked about my job as a journalist, and he appeared genuinely intrigued.

I felt myself relaxing as the conversation continued, and I thought to myself: Thank goodness, we appear to be hitting it off. The initial hiccup of finding a place to meet seemed to have dissipated, and was behind us now as things were going smoothly. Before I knew it, two hours had slipped by. I looked at my watch and told Robert I had to leave. I remembered telling Mike that I would be gone for only an hour. Robert seemed visibly disappointed. He looked at me, gave me a warm smile and said, "I'm really enjoying our conversation. Can you stay a little longer?" Hmm. "Yes!" It didn't take much to persuade me to stay!

Another half hour passed, and this time I told him I really had to go. I was concerned that Mike was home alone. I was only a few minutes away, but I didn't want to stay out too late, even though I knew that if Mike really needed me he would have phoned. Together, Robert and I left the hotel and walked back towards my house. I thanked him for a lovely evening and said that I looked forward to seeing him again soon.

At that point, Robert stood back and appeared to be quite taken aback by my comment. "Well, Emily ... yes, the evening went well, but can I let you know if I want to see you again?"

Huh? Now I was the one who was taken aback! "Oh ... well," I stumbled. "I guess ... I'm sorry ... I just thought we were both enjoying each other's company. I presumed you would want to meet up again." He didn't show much reaction, so I said, "Okay, well, then ... you take care. Goodbye." I walked away feeling somewhat confused.

As usual after a date, I pondered how it had gone. *We just had a three-hour date, and this guy wasn't sure if he wanted to meet again? That's it—no more online dating!* I came to the conclusion that I simply didn't understand the dating game. Being single and happy was far easier than trying to play stupid dating games. I was done with dating.

Chapter Seven

The Unravelling of Myrtle

A little over two weeks had passed since I had my Myrtle dream. I thought about the dream often, but as the days wore on, I began to wonder whether I would ever get to the bottom of the message. As it turned out, I didn't have to wait long at all.

The morning after my date with Robert, while I was at work, I received a text from him! Contrary to how the previous evening had ended, his message said that he'd enjoyed our meeting and would very much like to meet up again. *Whoa, here we go again.* My first thought was that he must be playing some kind of game. I'm hopeless at playing cat and mouse, and I wasn't sure how to respond to his text after feeling somewhat snubbed by him the previous night.

But again, something in my gut sang out and told me to just go with it. I replied, saying "Yes, okay, I'd like to meet again." He suggested we meet on the coming Thursday morning at 9.00am at a café in the city. When I arrived, Robert was already seated at a table. *Hmm, punctual again.* He was wearing a business suit because he was heading to work after our meeting. I was dressed a little more casually, as I was not working in the office that day.

We sat down for breakfast and fell easily into conversation. I learned that he had taken up tango dancing and that he loved everything

French—particularly French films. "What a coincidence; I'm taking French lessons at the moment," I said.

I'd studied French many years ago and thought it was time to brush up on the language. Although I wasn't into tango, I'd attended salsa classes the year before and had a lot of fun learning the dance. The conversation moved from France and dancing to spirituality. Robert reiterated what he'd told me on Sunday—that spirituality was important to him. We went on to discuss religions and beliefs. I found it easy to talk with him.

I'd been thinking about the Myrtle dream and its spiritual message, and although this was only our second meeting, I decided to tell Robert about my dream. I was concerned about what he might think of me. Would he think I was a wacky, esoteric, weirdo? As it turned out, he just listened. I could see from his expression that he was open to hearing about my dream. I recounted my story and relayed the words that I'd seen on the note.

Stay Myrtle.
Stay happy and contented.

I noticed as I said these words that Robert's facial expression suddenly changed. Right at the point of mentioning Myrtle and staying happy, I heard him gasp. His eyes filled with tears, and his jaw dropped a little. It was clear that he was filled with emotion. "What's wrong?" I inquired, wondering whether I was scaring him away. In the back of my mind, I thought I shouldn't have said anything. He sat quietly for a minute, and I could see he was digesting what I'd told him. He appeared to be shaken. After a few seconds, he said, "Have you heard of Myrtle Beach?"

"What? No, I haven't heard of Myrtle Beach." I was shaking my head and then I said, "Where is it? Is it here in Australia?"

"No, it's not in Australia."

"Are you sure you haven't heard of Myrtle Beach?" he insisted.

"Yes, I'm sure!" I said.

He said nothing for another minute, then suggested I Google it.

"What do you mean Google it? Why? What's there?" I asked.

Robert refused to comment any further other than to say that Myrtle Beach is in the US—in South Carolina. He urged me to Google "Myrtle Beach" once I got home. I was getting frustrated and intrigued and said I would do so. Robert then got up to leave for his meeting, but not before we made another date to meet in a couple of days. My thoughts were still on Myrtle Beach. Did South Carolina hold the answer to my dream? Why was Robert so emotional when I mentioned Myrtle and the words *Stay happy and content?* Did Robert hold the answer to my Myrtle riddle? My head was spinning with lots of questions. More than ever, I was determined to find the meaning behind it all.

I arrived home, rushed over to the computer and began Googling "Myrtle Beach". I found plenty of references to the beachside town on the east coast of America. I trawled various sites, but nothing jumped out at me. I discovered that Myrtle Beach is a holiday destination and is the golfing capital of the US. I gleaned that there were more than 100 golf courses in the area, but aside from this information, there was nothing particularly unusual about the place. From my initial search, I found that Myrtle Beach was a standard beach destination with all the trappings that accompany beach holidays. I was tempted to call Robert and tell him that I found nothing unusual about Myrtle Beach but decided against it. We were due to meet in a couple of days, and I would bring up the topic when I saw him.

Our next meeting was to take place in the newly renovated Sydney Hilton Hotel. We'd arranged to meet for a drink in one of the hotel bars before moving on to catch a live band. I arrived at the bar early and sat reflecting on the two meetings I'd had with my new-found American friend. Robert arrived shortly after, and I felt a sense of warmth emanating from him. He leaned over and kissed me on the cheek. I smiled at him, and we took our seats at the bar, where I immediately launched into my search for Myrtle.

"Robert, I've searched the internet for Myrtle Beach, and, to be honest, I couldn't find anything that resonated with me."

"Are you sure?" he said.

"Yes, of course I'm sure. What is it I'm looking for?" I was getting frustrated again. I don't know what I was expecting, but Robert told me he was heading to the US in June. "I'll be visiting my family and then travelling across the US and over to Myrtle Beach as part of the trip. The kids are coming with me."

"You're going to Myrtle Beach? Why didn't you tell me this before?"

"Because I'd only just met you, and when you told me about your dream and the meaning, I didn't know what to make of you. But I can see you really have no idea about Myrtle or any meaning behind it," he added.

"Why are you telling me this? What's at Myrtle Beach?" I asked.

"Emily, Myrtle Beach is a special place. There's a spiritual retreat there, and that's where I'm going." I didn't know what to say. A chill went right through my body. Even today, as I write this, I still get chills when I recall the moment he mentioned the retreat. "Have you heard of Meher Baba?" Robert asked me.

"Meher *what?* No, I haven't," I said.

"Meher Baba is an Indian spiritual leader; he died in 1969. He dedicated his life to serving others, especially the poor. Meher Baba established spiritual retreats all around the world, and I'm going to one in Myrtle Beach." My intuition suddenly hit red alert. Instinctively, I knew this was the Myrtle in my dream; it had to be, because the church in my dream represented a spiritual connection. I tried to pry more out of him, but he would say no more on the subject. He said that if I was genuinely interested in finding out more about this place, then I was to do my own research and learn about Meher Baba and his retreat in Myrtle Beach. I agreed. I was determined to find out more. Finally, my dream was starting to make sense.

The word after Myrtle had been obscured by the priest's finger in my dream. Now I had a very strong sense that the very first line of the message must have read or meant, *Stay at Myrtle Beach.* I was beginning to think that I may have to go there myself.

Chapter Eight

The Dream Becomes a Reality

Robert and I continued to see each over the following weeks, and with each week, our friendship intensified. I learned that Robert was born in California. When he was 12 years old, his family moved to a wine region called Sonoma. While attending the local school, he met Oliver, a fellow student. They became friends, and when Robert went to Oliver's house for the first time, he saw a tiny photo of a bearded man in Oliver's room. Robert told me that was the first time he'd seen a photo of Meher Baba. He asked Oliver who the man in the photo was. From that moment on, Robert became a Meher Baba follower and has been for 30 years. "I couldn't take my eyes off the man in the photo," he said. "I was so drawn to him."

In the late '90s, Robert visited Meher Baba's tomb in Meherabad, India. While he was there, he met an Australian woman who would later become his wife. After they married, they settled in Sydney. When the marriage ended, Robert decided to stay in Australia to be near his children.

A few weeks after our first meeting, Robert invited me to dinner at his place. Robert's home was a modern, two-bedroom apartment not far from the city centre. The suburb he lived in was a renowned cultural hub, filled with a multitude of restaurants, arts and music venues. And it was close to one of Sydney's major universities. When I entered his apartment, the first thing I noticed was the number of Meher Baba photos scattered around his home. Some of the photos were of Meher Baba standing alone, posing for the camera, while others were a close-up of his face. The pictures were either hanging on walls or standing on shelves. One photo in particular caught my eye.

This photo stood on a bookshelf and was about the size of a business card. I leaned to take a closer look. Meher Baba had a thick moustache and long, dark hair, which was tied back. The first thing I noticed was how kind and gentle he appeared. The smile on his face exuded so much warmth. I couldn't take my eyes off his face. I stood staring at the photo for some time before an overwhelming surge of emotion engulfed me. It felt as though a volcano of love was erupting deep inside me. I didn't understand how I could feel so much emotion about someone in a photo who I'd never seen or known. I'd never had this sort of reaction before. I was mesmerised by the picture. Underneath the photo was written, "*Don't worry be happy.*"

"Don't worry, be happy?" I inquired, looking over at Robert.

"Yes, that's Baba's quote," he said.

"Really, are you saying that Meher Baba was the originator of that quote?"

"Yep," he said.

As I looked closer, I read the full quote, which said, "*Do your best, then don't worry, be happy, and I will help you.*" It was signed Avatar Meher Baba.

"Tell me more about Meher Baba," I said. Robert gave me a look that said you have to do this on your own. "You need to find Baba yourself," he said.

"Baba?"

"Yes," he said, and then explained that "Baba" is the affectionate name used by many of Meher Baba's followers. They, in turn, are referred to as "Baba lovers". I felt that Robert was right about my finding out more on my own. I silently decided that yes, I would seek out this Baba person who'd captivated my interest. After all, I'd had the dream about Myrtle Beach, and I was sure there was a message for me that had something to do with this Meher Baba fellow.

I turned to Robert and said, "You know, I've already started my own research on Meher Baba, and there's a lot of information. I've looked at the website of the Baba retreat in Myrtle Beach. I think I have to go there." At that point, Robert reminded me that he would be travelling to the retreat with his children the following month. "It's our holiday, and I will be visiting my family, too," he added. He was planning to be away for a month. At no point had he asked me to join him, and I wasn't thrilled at the prospect of imposing myself on his family holiday. Yet, deep inside me, I had a strong sense that I would be going.

Changing the topic of his impending trip, Robert told me that Baba had many followers from around the world—even famous ones. "Really?" I said. "Like who?" Robert walked over to a large bookcase. On one of the shelves were dozens of albums and CDs stacked against each other. Alongside was a large stereo. He grabbed an album by Pete Townshend from the stack and said that Pete was a Baba lover.

"You mean Pete Townshend from The Who, the '60s rock band?" I asked.

"Yes. Do you like The Who or Pete's music?" he asked.

"Well, to be honest, I'm not familiar with many of their songs," I replied. "But there is one that's one of my all-time favourites: "Let My Love Open the Door." Robert agreed that it was a great song and said, "Pete has dedicated a number of songs to Baba; he even dedicated a whole album to him." And with that, he removed the record from the album cover and played several songs that Pete Townshend had written for Meher Baba. While we listened to the tracks, I watched Robert walk over to a cupboard. He opened the door, revealing dozens of books about Meher Baba. *Wow*, I thought. *Robert* is really *a dedicated follower*. I was astounded by the number of books he had on the man.

He brought several of them over to me. I grabbed one and flicked through a few of the pages, quickly trying to get my head around this Indian spiritual leader. I discovered that Meher Baba was born on 25 February, 1894, into a family of Persian descent. His birth name was Merwan Sheriar Irani, and he was educated in Pune, India. At the age of 19, he met Hazrat Babajan, an aged Muslim woman who was a renowned spiritually enlightened master.

It is said that Hazrat called out to the young Merwan as he rode past on his bicycle one day. He apparently went over to her, and she kissed him on the forehead. For the following seven years, Hazrat would help Baba find his spiritual identity. Meher Baba was born into a family of Zoroastrians—members of a pre-Islamic religion. As I was flicking through the pages, Robert told me that Meher Baba is also referred to as "The Awakener". I looked at him inquisitively. "Baba did not speak for the last 44 years of his life," he told me. "He chose not to utter a word because he said to his followers that so much has already been said in the past." Robert then told me that Baba had said, "I have come not to teach but to awaken. Understand, therefore, that I lay down no precepts."

"What do you mean he didn't talk right up until he died? Are you saying he didn't speak at all? How did he communicate?"

"He used an alphabet board," Robert said, then showed me a photo Meher Baba using the alphabet board. He pointed me to another Meher Baba quote in the book that explained why he took his oath of silence:

"Man's inability to live God's words makes the Avatar's teaching a mockery. Instead of practicing the compassion he taught, man has waged wars in his name. Instead of living the humility, purity, and truth of his words, man has given way to hatred, greed, and violence. Because man has been deaf to the principles and precepts laid down by God in the past, in this present Avataric form, I observe silence."

I found the information on Baba compelling. I also found that he passed away—or as Baba followers prefer to say, he "dropped his body" on 31 January 1969. This was all so new to me. I was somehow being drawn into a much more spiritual existence than the one I was currently living. My scepticism was still rife, yet this all felt so right to me and seemed to make sense.

I was relieved to learn that Meher Baba embraced all religions. From my point of view, the last thing I wanted was to discover that I was potentially becoming involved in a cult. But from the information that was coming to light, nothing could have been further from the truth. From what I could gather, Meher Baba was a selfless, compassionate soul. He spent much of his time working with lepers and the poor, providing food and medical care to needy villagers in India.

As the night wore on, I felt myself becoming more and more intrigued by Meher Baba ... and by my new American friend.

Chapter Nine

On the Road to Myrtle Beach

With only a few weeks to spare before his trip to the US, Robert talked to me more about his planned stay at Myrtle Beach. He would stay at the Meher Baba retreat for three days. It has a number of cabins, and he'd booked one specifically for his family; single people usually shared cabins, he told me.

The centre was founded in the 1940s when Meher Baba visited the region. Meher Baba told his followers that the retreat was to be built for all people and all religions. It was to be dedicated to individuals for rest, meditation and spiritual renewal. "The retreat is so beautiful; it's amazing and peaceful," said Robert. "The kids are going to love the beach; we're going to be down there every day." I listened quietly as Robert spoke of his love for Meher Baba. Then, out of the blue, he asked me if I'd like to come! I was genuinely surprised.

"Are you serious? You're really asking me to join you?"

"Yes, but please understand, I'm going there with my children, and you'll need to go on your own because it's the right thing for you?" He paused for a few seconds and then continued: "Of course, it would be great if you could come. You'll need to get a cabin on your own, as you won't be able to share with me," he said.
It seemed that suddenly my dream of Myrtle was making sense. It had

brought me to this man despite my thinking that I was through with dating. And now he was inviting me to join him on a spiritual retreat in Myrtle Beach. Maybe this was what the dream was all about … finding love?

Robert explained that couples may stay together in a cabin only if they are married. This rule was under strict instructions from Meher Baba. Single men and women who come to stay at any Meher Baba retreats are not permitted to share. Apart from the family and marital cabins, the accommodation was separated into women-only and men-only. For the first time since my dream, I now felt like the message was really starting to unfold. I'd felt sure I was going to visit Myrtle Beach as soon as Robert had mentioned it, but the complications of us not knowing each other for long had left me a little uncertain as to whether I should invite myself. But now, Robert had actually *asked me* to join him. I knew something bigger than me was unravelling before my very eyes.

I thought some more about the visit. At first, I didn't like the idea of sharing a cabin with anyone. I wanted to go to the centre to find answers for the book I was writing on the inner voice. I'd hoped to have a room of my own so I could write without any distractions. However, I thought a little more about the idea of sharing and reconsidered. It might be a good idea to share and learn about the experiences of other Baba followers. Robert reiterated that it was common for Baba followers to stay in shared quarters. He suggested I contact the retreat as soon as possible to see whether any vacancies were available, particularly as June is the start of summer in the US and is a busy holiday season.

Robert planned to spend the first part of his trip visiting family and friends and would be driving to Myrtle Beach on 25 June. With only a couple of weeks to go before he flew out, time was running out for me. I had to act quickly if I was going to organise my trip to coincide with his. The more I thought about this impending trip to the US, the more strongly I felt that I had to arrive in Myrtle Beach ahead of Robert. I had to go on this journey on my own and not be influenced by him. This was proving a challenge, because my feelings towards him were growing stronger each day. After some deliberation, I decided to arrive in Myrtle Beach one week ahead of Robert, which then gave me just one week to organise everything. I wanted to have a few days to be a tourist in South Carolina, before I headed over to the spiritual centre. And when Robert and the kids eventually arrive at the centre, we would have three full days together before I would head back home.

I had an overwhelming sense, or intuition, that I needed to be at the centre on 22 June, three days ahead of Robert. When I told him I would arrive at Myrtle Beach a week before him, he seemed a little surprised. I told him this would allow me to have a few days to do some sightseeing around South Carolina and Myrtle Beach. I'd never visited the east coast of the US, and it made sense to play tourist before heading to the retreat. I'd book my flights to arrive at Myrtle Beach on 19 June and then stay for nine days before returning home. I had one hurdle before I could leave: Could I get the time off work? Thankfully, I was able to get leave for a couple of weeks. I couldn't afford to take more than two weeks away from work or my sons.

When I spoke to my kids about my trip, my eldest son David encouraged me to go. He volunteered to take care of Mike for part of the time I was away, and Mike would spend the remaining time with his father. Slowly, things were falling into place, and my Myrtle escapade was starting to take shape. To the outside world, my trip to the US appeared rather sudden and indulgent. When I told my family and close friends about my trip, some were astonished that I would just take off and go because of a dream. I totally understood their reaction. Yes, it did sound crazy to take off on a whim. Yet everything inside me said that I had to go. More important, I felt I would get answers to help me write my book. Besides, I had to trust my own inner voice and take a risk if I was going to finish the book.

To help justify the expense, I wondered whether I might be able to earn some money to help pay for the trip by writing a travel piece on Myrtle Beach. After further investigation, I decided I'd write a story on Myrtle Beach and focus on the golf. Everything I'd read seemed to portray the place as a golf haven for fanatics. Perhaps an article on golf, along with a travel story, might appeal to one of the Australian golfing magazines? I didn't like my chances of pitching a story like this, but I figured that if I were given the opportunity to write this article, then it would be the confirmation I needed to go to Myrtle Beach.

I have always believed that when things line up easily and fall into place, you're definitely on the right track. So far, I'd managed to get a reasonably priced airfare to the east coast of America. I'd been granted leave from work at short notice. My sons were happy for me to take the vacation. And I was able to secure six nights' accommodation at the Meher Baba retreat. It had all happened so smoothly. Now all I had to do was secure a travel article and I would be 100 per cent convinced that I had to go.

On 14 June, a few days before I was to leave, I emailed the editor of *Golf Australia* to gauge whether his magazine might be interested in a US holiday golf story. It was a long shot. About an hour after I'd sent the email, I was surprised to find a response from the editor. I hadn't expected him to be working on a Sunday, let alone be receptive to my idea. I was overjoyed when I read that he would be very interested in a golf travel piece on Myrtle Beach. He wanted to run the story as a main travel feature and asked me to write 2,250 words; he would pay market rates. With this now confirmed, I felt sure I was on the right track. The money I would earn from writing the article would cover half of my travel expenses. Accommodation at the Meher Baba centre didn't cost very much, and I felt the trip was not going to be as expensive as I'd originally thought. It was all falling into place.

The following day, I contacted the Myrtle Beach travel and tourism authority. With little time before my arrival, I'd hoped to find someone who could provide me with information on the area. Unfortunately, I struck out and couldn't get help from anyone. I then contacted the US Consulate General in Australia hoping for help finding a person to act as a guide. The spokesperson from the consulate was very helpful and pointed me to a public-relations company in South Carolina. After a few more email exchanges, I arranged to meet Peter Welsh from the PR agency in Myrtle Beach. Peter would meet me on the second day of my trip. A couple of days later, he sent me an email detailing a list of places to visit that would help me write my story. Peter was a golfing fanatic and was looking forward to showing off some of Myrtle Beach's best golfing greens. With all the arrangements now made, I was well and truly on the road to Myrtle Beach. Wow!

Chapter Ten

Another Dream: Shantaram

It was hard to believe that only three months earlier I'd had a dream with a prophetic message. Now I was about to travel halfway across the world on a spiritual adventure looking for the answer. With only a couple of days before I was due to take off for the US, the reality of the trip was beginning to sink in. There were times I found myself feeling exhilarated by the prospect of going to Myrtle Beach and other times when I thought, *Am I crazy—travelling all this way because of a dream?*

And what of my connection to Robert? He appeared to have shown me the answer and was helping me unravel the Myrtle riddle. It was too much to comprehend. Although much of this was still a mystery, there was one thing I knew for sure: that after this trip, things were not going to be the same. Yes, I had some uncertainty about my trip, but I quickly dismissed any negative thoughts. It was too late for any trepidation on my part. The flights and accommodation were booked, and, thankfully, the trip was virtually paid for.

I turned my thoughts to the positive side. I'd scored a travel-writing gig! I'd wanted to become a travel writer for ages, so this was amazing. Really, at this point, I had nothing to lose but plenty to gain. And if I were to gain nothing out of the whole experience and receive no answer to my dream, at the very least, I'd have had a holiday and got to explore a part of the world that I'd never visited before. I'd also get the chance to spend a few days with Robert and his children.

During the couple of weeks before my departure, my relationship with Robert intensified; we became more than friends. We grew closer, and I felt myself falling for the man who was helping me unravel the Myrtle riddle.

The day before I was due to leave, I still wanted to find out more about Meher Baba. I spent several hours on the internet and found thousands of references to him, his quotes and his discourses. I learned that the name of this Indian mystic means "compassionate one" and that he is also known as the "Avatar". *Avatar* is a Sanskrit word meaning "descent of God". Despite following my intuition and booking the trip, my logical mind still didn't know what to make of all this information. The more I delved, the more questions I had. Could Meher Baba have sent the Myrtle message in my dream? And if he had, then why? And why *now?* I knew so little, and there was so much more to unfold.

As I trawled through dozens of websites and links to Meher Baba, I found myself fixated on photos of the man. Whenever I saw pictures of him, his face radiated a peace that I could tangibly feel. In many of his photos, he was surrounded by adoring followers. One photo of a young Meher Baba particularly caught my eye, because the face was strangely familiar. After further inspection, I stopped dead in my tracks because I realised this man had come to me in a previous dream! It was a dream I'd had a couple of months after my strange experience in Bali with Karen.

I remembered the dream:
I was sitting by a small stream surrounded by a wonderfully lush rainforest. The surroundings could have been Bali or any other tropical forest in the world. While I sat by the water, I heard footsteps approaching from behind. I turned around to see a young man. He had long, flowing dark hair and a moustache. His face had a youthful appearance that was gentle and kind. He was naked except for a white cloth, much like a sarong, that covered his hips.

As I looked over to him, he said, "I am Shantaram."

I responded by asking, "Are you my master?"

The man gave me a knowing look before he turned away and walked back into the rainforest. I got up quickly and said, "Stop! Wait! Who are you?"

But I'd already woken up.

I distinctly remember this dream because I'd written it down. After my experience in Bali, I had been shaken, and this dream had seemed prophetic, although I didn't know how. Like many of my dreams, I had written it down to keep a record and, I hoped, to decipher what it meant later. And now I was looking at the photo of a young Meher Baba, and I could see it was almost identical to the man in my dream who called himself Shantaram! Could Meher Baba have made his presence known to me much earlier in another dream? I'd dreamed about the Shantaram man almost two years earlier, but I hadn't known who he was.

At that moment, I felt a chill run up and down my spine, followed by goosebumps. Could this be another strange connection, or was it serendipity? Was something or someone trying to get a message to me? I couldn't shake the sense that there was a deeper meaning to all this. The more I looked at the photo of a young Meher Baba, the more convinced I was that he was the man from my dream. What on earth had Shantaram to do with Meher Baba, and Myrtle, and Robert? I didn't know what to make of all of this. My journalistic mind was asking all sorts of questions, so I decided to ask Robert whether the name Shantaram meant anything to him and if it had any relevance to Meher Baba.

At the time of my Shantaram dream, I didn't think too much about it. What *had* crossed my mind at the time was whether this Shantaram person might have been the spirit or entity who walked through me when I was in Bali. I know this might sound crazy, but having spoken to Vera and hearing her explanation that I had walked through another dimension, my mind was opening up to all sorts of ideas that my logical mind would otherwise negate.

The reason I thought the location in my dream was Bali is because it reminded me of the Balinese rainforest up in the mountains that Karen and I had visited during our time there. That and the fact that I'd had the dream not long after visiting Bali.

I quit my Meher Baba search and Googled "Shantaram". My search brought me to the book *Shantaram*, which had been written more than 10 years earlier. I dismissed the book search, because I couldn't see any connection or relevance. I tried other spellings of the name—Chantaram, Chantaran, and Shantaran—but all searches kept taking me back to the book. The search kept asking me: "Do you mean *Shantaram*?"

Hmmm … during my initial searches, I couldn't connect any of this to Meher Baba or my dream. I'd never heard of the book or its author. I dug deeper and found that *Shantaram* was written by Australian author, Gregory David Roberts. It was published in 2003, almost eight years before my dream. I found a synopsis of the book and learned that Roberts is a convicted Australian criminal who fled to India, where he wrote about daily life and the trials of living in Mumbai. The book gives readers a glimpse of his life during his time in the slums of Mumbai and his connections to the underworld.

Reading through the research, I couldn't see any relevance to my dream or Meher Baba. I wanted to find out what the word *Shantaram* meant. After a quick search, I found that it means "God of love". Well, this was interesting, because I'd heard Meher Baba being referred to as "God of love" and "all loving". *Now I was getting somewhere*, I thought. Perhaps there was a connection after all.

I had to get a copy of the book *Shantaram*, but I had little time: I was flying to the US the next day. I vowed to get a copy when I got home. Perhaps there was a message in the pages of the book or a connection to

India, the country in which it was set. One thing was for sure: At least one of the roads was leading me to India.

Chapter Eleven
Myrtle Beach and the Golfing Mecca

After travelling for almost 24 hours, I arrived in Myrtle Beach on 19 June. From the moment I stepped off the plane, a blanket of heat hit me. It was stifling. The day was a scorcher, with the Fahrenheit temperature well into the 90s. After leaving Sydney's winter, the temperature was a welcome surprise, though I hadn't anticipated such intense heat and humidity.

For the initial part of my stay I had booked a motel room right on Myrtle Beach itself. The hotel itself was uninspiring, its only asset was that it was perched right on the beach. My room was basic, but I had uninterrupted views of Myrtle Beach.

By the time I reached my motel room, it was close to 6pm, and the sun was beginning to set. I stepped onto the balcony and watched it slowly disappear, leaving behind a pink and golden haze across the horizon. For the first time in ages, I was alone. I was miles away from my children, my family and my friends. I stared across the ocean. *So this is Myrtle Beach ... the Myrtle in my dream.* I took a deep breath. *I am finally here.*

I ventured back into the room and jumped into bed. After the long flight and with little sleep in the past 24 hours, I was completely exhausted, and I quickly fell into a deep sleep. The following morning, I awoke at 5.30am. I was excited about being in Myrtle Beach and about being away from all the day-to-day stuff back home. I walked onto the balcony just as the sun was rising. The beach was empty, which gave me a chance to enjoy the view before the crowds congregated. I looked across to the ocean and inhaled the sea air. I stood there for a while, wallowing in the silence and enjoying the smell of the sea. I'd made arrangements to meet Peter my PR friend at 7.30am. With a couple of hours to spare, I turned on the TV and spent a little time surfing through the dozens of channels on American TV, only to find nothing worth watching. I got dressed, left the motel, and went for a walk to find coffee and something to eat.

Within a short 10-minute stroll from the motel, I found a Starbucks café. I ordered coffee and a pastry, which I enjoyed before returning to my motel to meet Peter. On the walk back, I wandered around the main drag hoping to find other cafés, but there seemed to be little in the way of cafés. When I got back, Peter was in the foyer. I guessed him to be in his mid-40s. He had a fair complexion and light-brown hair. He was dressed rather casually but explained that he was wearing his golf clothes in anticipation of the places we would visit. Over the next three days, Peter played host and took me to some of the best golf courses in the US. Peter was passionate about golf, and I found him knowledgeable and extremely generous with his time.

We visited a number of golf courses with glorious clubhouses reminiscent of a bygone era. South Carolina is noted for its old-world charm and stately manors. As I walked around the stately grounds, I could almost see the likes of Scarlett O'Hara and Rhett Butler dancing their way around the grand ballrooms as people had done over a century earlier. One clubhouse in particular—the iconic Pines Golf House—looked as though it was lifted right out of the movie *Gone With The Wind*.

In addition to its fantastic golf scene, Myrtle Beach's beaches and eateries had couples and families flocking to them. Peter told me that Myrtle Beach was one of the fastest growing family-vacation destinations in America, attracting almost 14 million visitors every year. He took me to a number of restaurants in the region. South Carolina cuisine seemed to be a melting pot of foods from all over the world, although it's still largely inspired by southern-style cooking and its Creole heritage. I have to admit that playing tourist and travel writer was fun. But at night when I was I was lying in bed, I would count down the days till I would reach the Meher Baba centre.

Finally, when 22 June came around, I couldn't wait to pack my bags. I'd made arrangements for a driver from the Meher Baba Centre to pick me up and take me to the retreat. At 11am, I stood at front of the motel, eagerly waiting for Patrick, the driver. When he turned up on time, I was so happy to see him that I jumped into the front seat quick smart. He was kind enough to take my bags and load them into the boot of the car. Patrick was one of those laid-back types who spoke quietly and had little to say unless I asked questions. He appeared to be a deep thinker.

We travelled down the busy highway for a short time before I struck up a conversation. Patrick began to open up a little more and asked me a few general questions, such as whether I'd been to the centre before. I told him I hadn't. He asked me why I'd come all the way from Australia. I told him that I'd had a dream with a message and that the message had led me to Myrtle Beach and Meher Baba. At first, he looked a little dismayed, but as I revealed more of my story, he seemed to understand and said that Baba comes to people in many ways. While Patrick drove along the highway, I was fixated on the US landscape. I watched dozens of cars whizzing by, and as I looked out the window, my eyes took in the sights. I noticed the vast number of billboards; they all seemed to be offering a promotion of some kind of place to eat.

We were now on the main road that would take us to the retreat. This stretch of highway was littered with fast-food outlets and megastores on one side of the road. On the other side, bushland stretched for miles and miles. Patrick said much of this bushland was dedicated to the Meher Baba centre. He began to slow down and turned onto a small dirt road leading into the woods. We travelled a short distance before reaching a set of large open gates. We passed through the gates and drove up to a cottage. Alongside the cottage was a small car park. Once Patrick parked, he told me to register at the cottage and that he would then drive me to my cabin. Apparently, the cabins were another kilometre down the road.

I walked over to the cottage to register and grab the key to my cabin. As I was walking back to the car, I glanced over to the gates we'd just passed through. It was then that the reality of where I was finally hit me. On the other side of those large gates were all the trappings of the Western world. The seductive outdoor billboards and the fast-food restaurants that represented the material world had come to an abrupt end once we'd passed through those gates. The images of the outside world gradually began to melt away. In their place, a new world was emerging. I'd left the West behind to immerse myself in Eastern culture. And who would have thought I'd do so right in the heartland of the American South? At first thought, Myrtle Beach seemed an unlikely place to discover an Eastern mystic, but I was yet to uncover more of the mystery.

I hopped back into the car with Patrick, and we drove down the track, which was surrounded by dense bushland and shrubs. Patrick drove slowly for the next five minutes. I had my window wide open and I could hear rustling in the nearby woods. Patrick told me it was likely a deer. I looked to see where the noise was coming from, and, just as Patrick suspected, a deer darted into the bush. I suddenly had a sense of what *Alice in Wonderland* must have felt like when she fell down the rabbit hole. I was having my own Alice moment.

As we drove towards my cabin, I was feeling elated at the prospect of what lay ahead. I felt a new door was opening for me, and it felt surreal and exciting at the same time. I was filled with happiness and a new-found sense of calm. As we approached the cabins, I saw the outline of a lake ahead. The sun's rays were bouncing off the water, making it sparkle. The first thing I noticed was how incredibly peaceful it was. Most of the cabins had a view of either the lake or the bush. "It's so beautiful," I whispered softly. All of a sudden, I was overwhelmed with emotions. I was overtaken by the same intense feeling I'd had when I first saw the photo of Meher Baba in Robert's apartment. I could feel my heart beating rapidly, and I was lost for words to describe the beauty and tranquillity I could both see and sense.

Patrick took my bag to a cabin which was perched on the water's edge. He turned to me, saying I was fortunate to have this particular cabin. "Why?" I asked. I recognised that it had an amazing water view, but he seemed to mean something else. He pointed to an old seat that was covered in a light, cushioned fabric. The seat was on the verandah—the perfect place to reflect while looking out to the water. "See that chair" Baba sat on that chair when he visited the centre," he told me. I looked over to the worn-out chair. I couldn't help but wonder how many other people had sat on it since Baba had opened the centre 60 years ago. "Oh! Well, I'd better sit on it for as long as possible while I'm here," I said jokingly. I walked over to the chair and sat down. I made sure I pressed my bottom down hard on the seat, hoping that some of Baba's essence would rub off on me.

Patrick left me to have some time on my own, so I sat on the chair a little longer and looked across the peaceful lake. It was easy to understand why this place was chosen as a retreat; serenity pervaded every inch of it. I couldn't believe how different I felt after being here for just a few moments. My life back in Sydney seemed like a million miles away.

When I registered at the office, I'd taken a brochure about the Meher Spiritual Centre. I grabbed the small leaflet and sat a little longer on Baba's chair. I read that the location was gifted to Meher Baba by Elizabeth Chapin Patterson, one of his American followers. The brochure was very informative. I learned that during the middle part of the last century, from 1931 to 1958, Meher Baba had wanted to establish links between the East and the West. He'd made many visits to Europe and the US and had many followers across the globe, including Elizabeth and Europe's Princess Norina Matchabelli. These two women became early disciples of Meher Baba. At some point, he'd asked them to find a location to build a retreat in the US. Apparently, he'd set a few conditions to finding the right piece of land. According to Baba, the land needed to have five qualifications:

The place must have an equitable climate, virgin soil and ample water. The soil must be able to become self-sustaining to a large number of people, and the property must be given from the heart.

After several unsuccessful attempts by the two women to find the right piece of land, the perfect location turned out to belong to Elizabeth's family. Her father, Simeon Chapin, and some of his business partners owned the land that I was then standing on. The land met all the criteria Baba had stipulated and was given to Elizabeth by her father. She then gave it to Baba "from the heart".

Chapter 12

The Meher Spiritual Retreat

It was 22 June, and I was at an idyllic location, sitting on a chair upon which the great Meher Baba himself had once sat. My cabin was very cosy; there was a small bathroom and two smallish bedrooms. Each room featured several photos of Baba. No matter what cabin or communal area I visited, there were always plenty of photos of Baba adorning the walls. His presence was ever shining down on his followers. The retreat itself drew beauty from every aspect of the bush, the lake and the cabins. All the cabins were quaint and decked out in comfortable furnishings.

As I rose from the chair on that first day, I watched a number of guests walking over to a large community room not far from my cabin. I stepped out onto the porch and received a warm welcome from several guests. We exchanged greetings, and they asked me to join them in the communal dining room to hear a talk by a man who'd met Meher Baba. Eager to hear more, I followed them into the centre. Thoughts of deadlines and global business news were far from my mind. I was totally at home in my new surroundings. The people were friendly, and I felt as though I could stay there forever.

When I entered the dining room, at least 20 people were sitting on an array of lounges and chairs. The furnishings gave the room character and warmth. The same could be said of the guests. Nervously, I walked into the room, not knowing what to expect. I found a seat and sat down. I turned to one of the guests and asked who was speaking. Bill Le Page, the person told me. Bill was an Australian man who'd spent quite a bit of time with Baba. I was surprised to learn that a fellow Australian was the guest giving today's talk. Just then, an elderly man who looked about 80 years old entered the room and took his place in front of the guests. Beside him was a woman who I later learned was his American wife, Diana. She was younger than him, with a slim build, and she seemed very elegant.

Bill addressed the audience, speaking of his time with Meher Baba. He explained that Baba had wanted him and his colleague, Francis Brabazon, an Australian poet, to build a spiritual centre in Australia. Bill shared his story and the frustration he'd felt while trying to spread Meher Baba's message throughout Australia in the 1950s and '60s. "We produced a small leaflet with Baba's message," he said. "We printed 60,000 of them, but we had very little response." Some 60 years later, I could still hear the heartache in Bill's voice at not being able to spread the message. It was clear that this had not been an easy job for the men.

As we listened to his story, everyone empathised with Bill's frustrations. We were disappointed to hear that Bill received little response after producing so many brochures. In the back of my mind, I was thinking about my dream and wondered whether it related to the message on the brochure. I asked Bill if he could recall what message been printed. "No," he replied. "It was so long ago—too long—I don't remember." Part of me had hoped that what had been written on the brochures may somehow be linked to the message in my dream. In hindsight, I know it was a long shot, but I thought it was worth asking.

After searching for an appropriate property, Bill and his colleague had eventually found two suitable locations for an Australian Meher Baba retreat. The spot would apply the same criteria as the Myrtle Beach location, meaning that the land had to be given from the heart. The properties they found were in Queensland and Sydney.

Nowadays, as Bill explained, he spent much of his time at the Meher Baba centre in Queensland, which had been named "Avatar's Abode". The retreat is on a 99-acre property at the summit of Kiel Mountain in Woombye, approximately 100 kilometres north of Brisbane. My journalistic sense, coupled with my increasing fascination with Meher Baba, was keen to learn more from Bill. We all sat for another hour while he spoke of his experiences, particularly those he'd had with the great man himself. I asked him what was the most memorable or defining moment that he'd had with Baba.

From the look on his face, I could see that was a hard question for Bill. He took his time before answering. "The first time I saw him, it was his eyes; they were so penetrating." He paused for a moment before continuing. "How could I ever answer that? In all the time I spent with him, they were *all* defining."

Despite my recent introduction to Meher Baba, what Bill was saying resonated with me. Just the few photos I'd seen had left me with a similar sense—that Meher Baba was someone very special. The part of me that would usually question and remain sceptical was all but gone. When it came to the man they called the Avatar, a strange sense of peace came over me.

After Bill had finished speaking, I went over to him to introduce myself. He and Diana were pleased to learn that another Australian was at the centre. The pair had already spent several months at Myrtle Beach. They planned to stay on and visit other Meher Baba centres in the US before going back home to Australia. They asked me what had brought me to the retreat. I told them I had come because of a dream. I recounted the dream and its message. Bill was intrigued and asked me whether I had visited Avatar's Abode in Brisbane. "No," I told him. "I'm new to all of this." I did tell him, however, that I was aware of the centre in Australia.

I went on to tell Bill and his wife that I'd come to the centre because I was writing a book. I was hoping to find some answers while I was at the retreat that would help me write it. I explained that the book would be on the power of the inner voice. In the back of my mind, while I was relaying this information to Bill, I was also questioning what all this meant. *Why was I here?*

Bill and Diana took an interest in the book and generously offered to help me with information on Meher Baba. I thanked them both and was about to leave when Diana mentioned she had a book that she thought would help me understand more about Meher Baba. She invited me to her cabin in the morning to pick it up. "It's written by a bunch of journalists who interviewed Baba on his visits to the West," she told me. It's called *Early Messages to the West.* Seeing as you're a journalist, you'll probably enjoy it more because they ask him lots of questions." "Sounds great," I said. Bill reminded me that he would be speaking again the following day and invited me to join them in the communal room. As I left the dining room, I looked around at some of my fellow guests. Everyone in the room appeared to have enjoyed Bill's account. It became obvious that anyone who'd met Meher Baba was held in high regard within the Baba community, particularly if they were given tasks from the master, as Bill had been.

I made a mental note to attend the next gathering and to hear more about Bill's time with Baba. Unbeknown to me, it was at this next gathering that I would meet a young Australian man who would add another twist to my Myrtle dream.

Chapter 13

Janine

I've already admitted that I'd never been on a spiritual retreat before setting foot in the Meher Baba centre. As I walked back to my cabin, I thought about how I was halfway across the world at a spiritual centre all because I had taken a leap of faith and followed my instincts. By my very nature as a journalist, it's normal for me to ask questions and remain impartial—even sceptical. On this occasion, I'd made a pact with myself to keep an open mind to see what I could learn at the Meher Baba centre.

My religious belief is that we are equal. I think that everyone is entitled to their beliefs as long as they do not force their views on others. Spirituality and religion can bring people together. This became apparent through the people I met at the Meher Baba retreat, including Helena, with whom I shared my cabin. Helena was a schoolteacher of German origin and was not a Meher Baba follower, although she said she respected his teachings. She came to the centre each year during her summer school break to de-stress and rejuvenate. Helena simply enjoyed the spiritual aspect and didn't hold any strong religious beliefs. It didn't matter to her that I was Catholic, and it wouldn't have mattered if I were any other religion, either. We were all here to grow spiritually.

At the centre, there were Catholics, Jews, Buddhists and people from just about every religion from all over the globe. Some were there on a pilgrimage; others, like Helena, had come to unwind. Some came with families for a holiday. I hadn't come to the retreat looking to find a new religion. I had come hoping to gain insights into my intuition and to find the answer to my Myrtle dream. During my time at the retreat, I never had any sense of being sucked into a cult or any other ritual from which I couldn't escape. I quickly dismissed any fears I'd had of falling into a New Age religion.

Meher Baba himself had made it clear that he belonged to no *one* religion. This, he said, was his universal appeal to all people. A lovely quote of Baba's summed it up for me:

"I am not come to establish any cult, society, or organisation, nor even to establish a new religion. The religion that I shall give teaches the knowledge of the One behind the many."

Aside from the Catholics, Jews and Buddhists who followed Baba, other people, including Muslims, Zoroastrians, and even those who considered themselves atheists and agnostics seemed to love Meher Baba and his teachings. From what I'd witnessed, we all wanted to share in Meher Baba's philosophies on life, love and service to others. We had come from all walks of life: There were doctors, lawyers, homemakers, single people, couples and families. We'd come to connect spiritually, not only with Baba and his loved ones, but also with each other and, most important, with ourselves.

I'd been at the centre for only a couple of days, but there was really something quite magical about this land and the lake. The retreat exuded purity and peace; on the other hand, there was also a distinctly powerful presence in the air. The presence wasn't invasive nor frightening. Quite the contrary—it was powerful in the sense that it allowed me to feel free. Being there, I felt free from worry and from the trappings of the material world. It was a feeling I'd never experienced before. I'm certain that the other guests felt the same, and it seems to have happened the moment we passed through the main gates. The transformation was visible, as I witnessed long after I arrived home. I'd had a few photos taken of myself while I was at the retreat and a few weeks later, when I saw them, I swore I looked 20 years younger! It was as if the stress and worry had been wiped off my face. I knew it had something to do with being in such a pure environment.

At the retreat, serenity permeated the property and had the same impact on the centre's volunteers and employees. I was struck by their gentle natures and kindness, not only towards guests but also towards each other. Nothing appeared to rattle them. They spent much of their time attending to their chores with love and devotion. They appeared mindful that everything they did was for Meher Baba.

If I'd ever wanted to meet a real live angel, then Janine—one of the Baba employees—came close. Janine did jobs with ease and grace. It didn't matter what time of day I saw her: She always had a smile on her face. She reminded me of the Mona Lisa, because her smile was a permanent fixture. Her fair hair was often tied back, accentuating her delicate facial features. During my time at the centre, I'd regularly catch Janine in the kitchen with a couple of helpers cooking meals for everyone at the centre. She gave this gesture freely and with generosity. Guests of the centre are expected to supply their own food. The retreat has two large communal kitchens that guests can use to cook and store their food. But so often, there was Janine, cooking for all.

Meal times at the retreat were my favourite because of the communal efforts of everyone staying at the centre. It didn't matter who was cooking; whether it was the guests or the employees, the food and conversation made for a united experience. At times, there would be 20 or 30 of us seated around the table sharing food. Everyone loved Janine, so it's no surprise that I was drawn to her, too. I looked forward to any opportunity to spend time with her, even if it was for only a few minutes between her chores.

Janine and I quickly became friends. What I found so fascinating about her was that she seemed to have an in-built antenna or radar: Whenever I wanted to find her, she would appear out of nowhere. I never had to look far before she would surface. Bear in mind that the retreat spanned acres, and at the height of the holiday season, the centre has a couple hundred people staying there at any given time. The cabins have no phones, nor is there any signal for mobile phones or computers unless you left the property. There was a phone in the communal kitchen for emergencies. Trying to reach someone within the retreat was pot luck. But whenever I wanted to get a hold of Janine, she would appear. The same thing would also happen with Robert once he arrived. Whenever I wanted to get a hold of him, he'd just appear.

Janine and I would often joke about this connectedness. She said that when I returned to Australia, I would have to use the "inner-net". This was her term for connection, a play on the word internet. "Use the inner-net, Emily. That's how we'll connect," she'd say to me a few times. Janine did not have internet access or a mobile phone; instead, she chose to live a simple life dedicated to Baba and the centre. After spending time with Janine, I began to wonder whether angels in human form really do exist! It reminded me about the woman who'd approached me in the bookstore all those months ago.

Chapter 14

Another Myrtle!

During my stay at the centre, I found it hard to sleep. I would toss and turn for hours before finally drifting off—sometimes not until well after midnight. I attributed this to jetlag, though the lack of sleep never hindered my energy. I was fully alert yet peaceful, which almost didn't make sense. But that's truly how I felt.

Each morning, I awoke eager to learn more about Meher Baba, and every day when I stepped outside my cabin, the sun's rays would beat down heavily. It was hot and humid. The weather reminded me of summer in Sydney, where the air can be thick and still from the day's scorching temperatures. One particular morning, I got up and walked down to the lake before breakfast. I grabbed my camera to take photos of the lake in the early hours; I wanted to capture all its beauty and stillness.

When I arrived at the lake it was eerily quiet. Most of the guests were still sleeping. I walked to a small bridge that linked both sides of the retreat. Under the bridge, a gentle stream flowed freely. I looked out at the lake and noticed a small dinghy with a couple of people in it. I took hold of my camera and was preparing to take photos when out of the blue, a young Indian man came running over to the bridge.

He was in a state of panic and appeared to be calling out to the people in the boat. I walked closer to the bridge and on further inspection, I saw what was causing his alarm. Circling the small dinghy was an alligator! The couple was clearly traumatised as they watched the alligator inch itself closer to their boat. The man called out to the couple and told them to remain calm and start rowing back to land. "Oh my God," I said. "I'll run to get help." The man ignored me and kept calling out to the couple. "Don't move out of the boat! Stay down! Don't stand up!" he yelled at them. He then turned to me, "That's my wife and her friend!" he said.

The couple stayed where they were and too frightened to move while the alligator sniffed around. Several minutes later, the alligator must have sensed their immobility due to their having remained calm. The creature eventually retreated. The couple hastened their paddling and rowed back to shore. Just before the alligator moved out of sight, I grabbed my camera and took a photo. I managed to get a photo of the alligator's head rising above the water only a few metres away from the boat! It was an impressive picture: the small boat all alone on the lake, except for the alligator, which was too close for comfort.

Once the boat was safely back on shore, I decided I'd had enough excitement for the morning and made my way back to my cabin. I dropped the camera in my room and grabbed a list of activities taking place at the centre. I glanced at the page, hoping to attend several of the events.

June 22 to 29 Programs

Wed	*3.00pm*	Informal Gathering with Bill Le Page (sharing Baba stories)
Thu	*8.00pm*	Music Concert Library Reading Room
Fri	*8.15pm*	Guest Speaker Meeting Place
Sat	*3.00pm*	Readings from Mehera-Meher: A Divine Romance Library Reading Room
Sat	*8.15pm*	Film of Meher Baba Lord of Love 4 short films Meeting Place
Sun	*8.00pm*	Celebrating the Divine: Share poetry, stories and other creative expressions of the heart Library Reading Room
Mon	*3.00pm*	Informal Gathering (sharing Baba stories) Original Kitchen
Mon	*8.00pm*	Discourse Meeting Library Reading Room
Tue	*8.00pm*	Music Concert Library Reading Room

I read through the list of events and decided that I'd attend the music concert that evening. I left the cabin and headed to the kitchen. On my way, I joined other guests making their way to breakfast. Breakfast usually consisted of coffee or tea, cereal, toast, jam and a variety of other tasty spreads. Hot food was prepared and shared by everyone. The best part of this experience was being part of the conversations around the breakfast table. I learned that most of the people at the retreat were American, although there was a smattering of other nationalities, including German, Indian and a few Aussies.

Within a short time, word had spread through the centre that an Australian journalist had travelled halfway across the world because of a dream. Some people found this concept amusing. Some could not fathom taking such a risk and spending so much money on a whim because of a dream. Despite that, many of the guests told me that the more they thought about how Baba comes into people's lives, the more they understood. Invariably, they would then give me a look of knowing, as if to say, "Yes, this is Baba working his way to get to you".

Everyone had a "Baba story". I enjoyed listening to the many ways Baba came into his follower's lives. Some people, like Robert, had been Baba lovers for many years. Some had known Baba all their lives because their parents were followers. And here I was, a latecomer to Baba on the wrong side of 40. I was miles from home and had come here on the basis of a dream. Initially, I felt like the odd one out. Yet as the days went on, I was becoming more and more comfortable in my decision to come to Myrtle Beach.

That afternoon at 3pm, I made my way to the communal kitchen to hear the next instalment of Bill Le Page's time with Meher Baba. Janine was making her way there, too. She walked over to me and asked whether I'd like to share my story of how I came to Baba. "Tell them about your dream," she said in her sweet, delicate voice. At first, I wasn't sure about getting up and speaking in front of everyone, but she insisted. Bill also encouraged me. I eventually agreed, although I preferred to remain seated while I told the story. Everyone listened intently, and some were quite surprised to hear Baba's message in a dream.

Stay Myrtle ...
13 days ...

Somebody repeated the line and asked me whether I had heard of Myrtle Beach before the dream?
I told them emphatically that I hadn't.

"No, not at all, I have never heard of Myrtle Beach."

Stay Myrtle ... stay contented and after 13 days, see what happens.

As I recounted the dream, I was thinking about what might happen after 13 days here at Myrtle Beach. Someone in the audience echoed my thoughts. "You'll have to wait to see what happens in 13 days." I agreed, nodding my head. After I'd finishing relaying my dream and answering a few questions, a young man with blond hair raised his hand to get my attention. He appeared to be in his mid-20s. He stood up and introduced himself. The first thing I noticed was his distinct Australian accent. He had a soft voice, and there was a gentleness about him. "Hi Emily. My name is Chris, and I work at Avatar's Abode, the Meher Baba centre in Woombye, Queensland."

He said he was a builder and had been working on a new kitchen for the centre. I nodded to him and said, "Oh, wow, how wonderful to have another Aussie here. Hi Chris." Janine piped up and commented that there were now five Australians at the retreat. I gathered it was unusual to have this many Aussies at the centre at once. Bill nodded to Chris, and the men exchanged greetings, as they were obviously well acquainted with each other. Chris asked me whether I had visited Meher Baba's retreat at Woombye. I told him I hadn't.

Chris then posed another question, the answer to which would not only stun the audience but also leave me speechless. "Emily, do you know what 'Woombye' means?" I was trying to understand what all this had to do with my story about Myrtle. I replied that I had no idea and asked him why he'd asked me that question. Bill and Diana were paying close attention to Chris, too; as they did not know the meaning of "Woombye" either.

"'Woombye' is an aboriginal word for myrtle. Black myrtle," Chris said with genuine amusement and a smile on his face. Everyone in the room gasped. I shook my head in disbelief and shock.

"No! Come on Chris, you're fooling with me. No way! Are you saying there are now two myrtle connections to Meher Baba?" Bill shook his head in astonishment. Both he and Diana were speechless. "Chris, are you sure?" I asked. Bill let out a sigh and said he'd had no idea that Woombye meant Myrtle. Chris confirmed that it did. "Yes. There's a café in Woombye called Black Myrtle Café. That's where I heard it first. The owners named their café after Woombye, the aboriginal word for black myrtle," he said. My head was spinning. OMG! Now there was *another* Myrtle!

This reaffirmed *everything*. I felt justified in following my initial instincts when Robert first spoke of Myrtle Beach, and now there was no doubt left in my mind that this, Myrtle Beach, was the Myrtle in my dream. I absolutely believed that Meher Baba was behind my Myrtle dream. It was too bizarre to have Myrtle in two locations associated with him. Everyone in the room was speechless. As far as we could determine, no one had ever made the Myrtle connection between the two locations. After digesting this news a little, I again questioned Chris: "Are you sure, Chris? I have to do a search when I get back to a computer. I need to know if 'Woombye' really *does* mean 'Myrtle.'

"I'm certain,' he said.

I joked, adding, "For goodness sake, I could have flown to Queensland instead of halfway across the world and saved myself a heap of money!" Everyone laughed.

Once the meeting was over, I went back to my room. I thought more about the synchronicity of events. Had I not been in the same room to share my story with Chris and Bill at that time, none of us would have been any wiser about the connection between the two Myrtles. The Woombye-Myrtle link added another dimension to my dream and to this journey. I couldn't wait to tell Robert!

Just before getting to my cabin, Janine called out to me. She ran over and said that I must go to India and visit Meher Baba's resting site in Meherabad. I let out a deep sigh—first America and now *India?* Reluctantly, I answered, "Yes, I know. Some day I will go." This was not the first time someone had encouraged me to go to India. Robert had also urged me to go. The question of visiting India was never far away when any Baba followers learned that I was a newcomer. But I have to admit that the topic of India was becoming a bit of a bugbear for me. It's not that I didn't want to go, It's just I had no desire to go right now. I would prefer to take a trip to India when it felt right for me, rather than to appease others. Followers of Baba are always encouraged to visit his tomb, but for me, I wasn't quite ready to go.

The pressure to travel to India had caused some friction between Robert and me. He couldn't understand why I didn't want to go. There was no doubt in my mind that visiting Baba's resting place would be a significant event in my life, but I figured I would go when I was ready. One day, out on one of my early morning walks, I asked Baba to help me understand why I don't want to go to India. In my mind, I said to Baba, "You've given me messages before. Why do I have no desire to go to India?" In the stillness of the early morning and in the very depth of my subconscious mind, I heard a steady, strong voice say to me, "You will go to India when I tell you to go." That's when I got it.

Travelling to India had nothing to do with Robert or anyone else wanting me to go. I was still coming to grips with all of this. If I needed to explore my spirituality further, then I would go to India, but for now, this was already a big journey for me. How going to India would eventuate, I wasn't too sure. But what I was sure of was that I had to trust that the time would come. A question that continually crossed my mind since I had connected my dreams to Meher Baba was *Why?* I also wondered, *Why now, at this stage in my life?* I'm still unsure of the answer to that one!

Chapter 15

What is Intuition?

My thoughts continued to wander back to my chance meeting with Chris. I was beginning to feel overwhelmed by the sequence of events. The coincidence of Chris being in the same room while I recounted my Myrtle dream was remarkable, or maybe it was just serendipity again. I seemed to be experiencing serendipity more and more.

That night, I once again lay awake for hours, tossing and turning. So much had happened over the course of two months—all because of one dream. When I looked back, I recalled how it started with a last ditch attempt at online dating, which in turn led me to Robert, who in turn would help me unravel the Myrtle prophecy. Then I would discover that he held the missing piece from the first line in my dream: *Stay Myrtle [Beach]*.

The missing word now made sense. I was convinced that *Myrtle Beach* had to be the words in the first line of the message that the priest had shown me. Now, after taking another gamble to travel to the US, I'd found more pieces to the Myrtle puzzle. I began to wonder more and more about the power of the human mind. What really happens in the subconscious, and what, particularly, occurs when we are sleeping and dreaming? I was spending time thinking about the power of dreams and about other people who'd had significant dreams. I remembered reading that Beatles legend Paul McCartney's hit song "Yesterday" came to him in a dream.

When I cast my mind back to when I'd first set about writing this book, I recalled making several attempts to begin the story. But each time, I wasn't happy with the direction it was going. I'd toyed with the idea for almost four years, but the book had never come together as I would have liked. I purposely didn't want to write a how-to book on intuition, because so many are already out there that have been written by people far more experienced than I am. I knew the best way for me to tackle this subject would be by example—in other words, by sharing my real-life experience. I had also considered my options concerning who would publish such a book, because it differed greatly from my other books on money and wealth. When Random House published my first book, *The Money Club,* the editor, Rachel said she liked the idea because it was based on real-life experiences. "People learn from others who are just like them," she told me.

The Money Club is about my experiences and those of my fellow female investors. The book tells the story of how we started an investment club that grew from our initial idea of holding a book club. We were ordinary women: Some of us had families, and some of us were single, but what we had in common was a desire to secure our financial future. We were not financial experts. Our aim was to learn about investing as a group, and we became quite successful at it. That story resonated with many people, particularly women, who wanted to become financially independent. The book became a bestseller, largely due to the accessibility of the information based on my real-life experiences.

Following my intuition is at the heart of *this* book. So, if I am to trust my intuition and write on this subject, then I needed it to take its form from a personal perspective.

How Does Intuition Work?

I am going to keep it simple. Intuition is the small voice that nags you to make a decision or take action. More often than not, we choose to ignore it – usually because the course of action or decision may not bring us our preferred outcome. Ultimately, that decision will always turn out to be the right one if you make a decision based on what brings the most peace of mind to a situation.

You will know when you have taken the right course of action simply because you feel it physically.

On the other hand, when you make a decision based on what you would *like* the outcome to be or make a decision to appease other people, such as a loved one, then you can often feel anxious about that decision. When you feel a sense of foreboding or anxiety, it's the body's way of letting you know that you're not on the right path.

Don't expect your intuition to bloom overnight. In my experience, it takes time to get to a stage of living intuitively. But once you learn to listen to and trust your intuition, a sense of calm does take over. You'll also feel more confident in the choices you make. This is something I have experienced time and time again.

Your inner voice is the one thing you can trust. That voice is your higher self, and nobody in the world wants the best for you more than you do. So first and foremost, trust yourself. The inner voice is always broadcasting. All you have to do is listen to that powerful voice within you.

Take this example: Your intuitive voice is telling you that your partner is cheating on you. Although you have no evidence, there is a nagging feeling inside that will just not let up. When you decide to take action and ask your partner directly, you find that you were right. Your intuition will always alert you to something that is not right. The best course is to act on that nagging inner sense. Please note: Intuition is different from being jealous or controlling of your partner. Jealousy comes from feeling insecure, whereas intuition is a deep knowledge that something isn't right.

Another example might be that you feel you need to leave your job and find another one. Once you do so, you love the new job, and you're much happier. Down the track, you might hear from your former colleagues that the job you left became redundant and that you would have risked losing your job if you'd stayed. This happened to me. I had a great job, but I wasn't happy. My logical mind was telling me to stay because it is near impossible to get a good job in media like the one I had. On the other hand, my heart was telling me I wasn't happy and that it was time to leave. For several months, I agonised over the decision. I eventually took the risk and left the job, knowing that the prospects of getting more work in media were dire. I decided to try my hand at freelance writing and set out to finish this book. I'm glad I did. A few months after I left, things took a turn for the worse at my previous job. Some of my colleagues were made redundant, while others took severance packages. Leaving when I did allowed me time to establish myself as a freelance writer. Had I waited and left when everyone else did, I might have faced far more competition.

Your intuition is a call to action, and it creates an awareness of a certain situation. When you make the decision to leave a destructive marriage or an untenable job, in your heart you know you have to act, because you can sense that the uncertainty of the situation you are in will eventually destroy you. It's a tough decision to make, but once you come to terms with it, a sense of peace overcomes you.

That's not to say that the road ahead will always be rosy; of course, it may not be, because we need time to heal from situations, such as leaving a relationship or a toxic workplace. But once you do, you know that you've taken the right path. So it's worth saying that the more you use your intuition, the more you will come to know the difference between it and your thoughts. When you follow through on your gut instinct—even when the odds are stacked against you—that's when you find the truth. Intuition is an inner sense that taking a turn against the wind feels more natural than being blown along.

When you start making choices that initially seem counterintuitive, it's common to come across naysayers. Often, these people have your best interests at heart, but their negativity is based on fear. They will criticise your decision to leave a marriage when they do not fully understand what is going on. You might also have people urging you to stay in your job, but they are not aware that every day, your self-esteem is being crushed or you are being bullied at work. And more to the point, they cannot feel what is inside your heart that's telling you to change tack.

It takes courage to listen to your heart and have faith in yourself. Your inner voice is calling out to you all the time; it wants you to take a certain path or action that it knows will lead to the greatest outcome. To follow that voice, you have to learn to back yourself. After a few times following your heart, you'll realise that when you do, things always turn out well. Trusting your intuition is a confidence-builder.

Meditation is a wonderful way of tapping into your inner voice. You don't have to completely shut down your mind, and you don't have to sit still for hours. Meditation helps you hear what your inner voice is telling you. It helps you tap into that inner compass. Most of us rush around ignoring our thoughts when really we just need to address them. Meditation is not meant to be difficult; it's meant to be easy.

If you're finding it hard, then you are trying too hard. Just let your thoughts come through. Let them run through your mind, because underneath them is where you will find the answers to any questions you are asking. It's not so much a case of trying to shut off your thoughts; it's more about letting them through but not getting involved in a whole dialogue with them. Just let them pass through. That's all meditation needs to be. You'll soon begin to realise which thoughts require action.

I work from home these days, but when I was still working in an office, I often used meditation during my lunch hour. Whenever I was under pressure to meet a story deadline, I'd take a few minutes away from my desk, find a quiet spot and meditate. In the days when I was working for a business magazine, I sometimes walked out of the office and down to a nearby pier; I'd close my eyes and focus on calming my thoughts. I would keep my eyes closed for as long as possible to shut out any distractions. I'd often be there for only five or 10 minutes, but this brief escape always helped me gather my thoughts.

When you need to make a decision and you feel your mind is playing tag between your head and your heart, you will feel a sense of anxiety. The best thing to do is to go back and focus on the heart or intuition. You'll know when you have tapped into the intuitive voice, because you'll feel a huge sense of relief.

It's important to understand that intuition can really go off the rails if you're under constant stress. Again, this is when meditation can help. My intuition is always at its purest and best when I'm in a regular meditation routine. And by this I don't mean meditating for hours, because the reality is, how many people can afford that kind of time? Ten minutes a day is great. It's even better if you can do 10 minutes when you first wake up the morning. I find that the morning is best because my thoughts are calmest. It's easier to tap into the subconscious mind when you first wake up because you are still fresh from sleep and your mind hasn't yet been bombarded with daily messages and stuff to do.

Meditating before you go to bed is also great, as it will help you get a better night's sleep. Whenever I struggle to sleep, I meditate for a little while until my mind has calmed. Then I write down what is worrying me, and I say to myself: *It is now time to sleep. It's late, and there is nothing I can do till tomorrow, so there is no use worrying.*

It's worth saying that the terms "inner voice", "instinct" and "intuition" all imply the same thing. Meher Baba nails the feeling of intuition with the following quote, which I love:
"When you feel something as intuition and have no doubt about it, then know it is real. Passing doubtful thoughts and temporary emotional feelings should not be given importance. But when you feel it touches your heart, follow it.
"When it is from the mind, it is not intuition. Intuition means 'that which comes from the heart'. In the divine path, first there is intuition, then inspiration, then illumination, and finally realisation. If it touches your heart, follow it. And God willing, from today you will know that if it is intuition it is right."

To summarise, the conscious mind will almost always try to override the intuitive voice. It takes immense courage to listen to your intuition and act on it, especially when taking that action seems to go against everything that makes sense. When we learn to trust our hearts and listen to our intuition, the results will be obvious. As I mentioned earlier, following your inner voice takes courage, and it takes time and practice before it becomes second nature and overrides your conscious mind—those thoughts we most commonly follow.

I encourage you to stick with it and practice listening to your inner voice; once you master this technique, it will become an invaluable gift that you can use to benefit every area of your life.

Chapter 16
Memories of Myrtle

On day three at the retreat, I was so excited because Robert was due to arrive. It had been almost three weeks since I'd seen him back in Australia. I spent much of the day attending activities at the centre. Between programs, I went down to the beach. On the outskirts of the retreat, a sandy trail led down to the sea. The exclusivity of the centre meant that the only people who frequented this part of the beach were guests. Again, the temperature was scorching, making the beach the best place to cool down. During my stay at the centre, I spent a lot of time walking along the beach, talking to other guests and listening to their experiences with Meher Baba.

After spending three full days at the centre, I was feeling incredibly light. By this I mean that my thoughts were clearer. Even the way I walked felt much lighter than when I'd first arrived. I felt as though I was walking on air! I was having a great time, and I felt so light and joyful. I often felt as though my feet didn't touch the ground. I guessed that this was part of the appeal of a spiritual retreat, spending time in this place, where the environment is so pure.

I made an effort to eat well while I was there. I felt it would be a crime to pollute my body with unhealthy food given where I was staying. I believe it was the combination of healthy food going hand in hand with such a pure lifestyle that led to the wonderful feeling of lightness. The food at the centre was incredibly healthy. Most of the guests had brought food that was organic and fresh. We dined on wholemeal breads, nuts, fruits, organic jams and honey; even the desserts and snacks were healthy. I looked forward to every meal, knowing that it would be tasty and healthy. I was hoping that Robert would arrive in time for the evening meal that night, but as I'd had no contact with him for a week, I wasn't sure whether I'd see him.

As it turned out, we bumped into each other that day! I thought about the term "divine timing", because our bumping into each other would happen over and over again during our time at the retreat. Whenever I wanted to contact Janine, Robert or anyone else, they would just appear. I was constantly amazed by this timing. I reasoned that it must have something to do with the clarity of my thoughts—either that or something telepathic was going on!

A concert was scheduled in the library reading room for the night Robert was due to arrive. The performance was to begin at 8pm and finish around 10pm. I wanted to catch the performance, but doing so meant I may miss seeing Robert if he did turn up. If this were the case, I would have to wait until the following day to catch him. As I made my way to the concert, I realised that I'd forgotten my torch. It was critical to carry a torch at night; it was virtually impossible to see your way around the centre without one. For the most part, the centre was pitch black once the sun had set. The last thing I wanted to do was stumble around in the dark trying to find my cabin. So with only a few minutes to spare before the concert, I ran back to grab the torch.

As I was nearing my cabin, I saw a tall man walking away—it was Robert! I hastened my pace and ran over to him. I figured he must have just arrived and had come looking for me. "Robert!" I yelled out. He turned around and smiled. 'Oh there you are," he said. I hugged him tightly. It felt so good; I really had missed him. He pulled away from me and looked at me for a few seconds before commenting, "You're glowing!" The statement came as a surprise because for much of my time at the retreat, I wore no make-up. My dark hair was usually pulled away from my face, tied in a ponytail. However, a day in the sun and a light tan had given me some colour. Upon reflection, I realise that the glow that Robert referred to wasn't just an external glow; it was an internal glow, and it emanated from everyone. When I look back at photos of myself during my time at the retreat, I can see it—not just on *my* face but on the faces of the other guests, too. "It must be this place!" I said. "It's so good see you. I've forgotten my torch. So I was running back to the cabin. It's just as as well, because otherwise I wouldn't have caught you until tomorrow."

Robert had just arrived, and his children were in their cabin unpacking. I told him I was on my way to the concert and asked whether he wanted to join me. "Sure. I'll go back to the cabin and get the kids and we'll see you there." We arranged to meet outside the concert room and go in together. By the time we got there, most of the other guests were already seated. It was an informal gathering, with people sitting on cushions on the floor or on sofas and chairs forming a circle around the musicians. The performers that night were a duo and they sang folksy devotional songs for a couple of hours.

Robert and his children enjoyed the performance. Once the concert ended, Robert made his way around the room greeting some of his old friends. The drive from his family's home to the centre had taken him most of the day, and his children were tired from the long journey. Robert was going to head back to the cabin and get the kids to bed. I wished them all good night, and we made plans to meet in the kitchen for breakfast the following morning.

Chapter 17

Thirteen Days and Another Revelation

After another night of choppy sleep, I awoke knowing that Robert had arrived and that we were going to have some time together. He'd made it clear to me that while he was at the centre, his main priorities were to reconnect with his spiritual side and to spend time with his children. I was mindful of not invading his space and was happy to catch up with him whenever it felt right. I was enjoying my time at the centre so much that it didn't matter if I spent it with him. I loved interacting with the other guest and locals. With only three days left before I had to return to Sydney, I was determined to enjoy every minute of this idyllic place.

The next morning, I was already in the kitchen when Robert and the children arrived. Breakfast was being served, and the table was full of familiar faces. When Robert entered, he received a warm greeting from the guests. Despite his initial suggestion that he wanted to spend quality time with just his children, we all ended up spending a lot of time together. We went down to the beach at every opportunity and shared meals with some of the other guests. Every moment was taken up, and the time flew by far too quickly for my liking. The next day, I recounted the Woombye-Myrtle connection to Robert. He found it just as hard to believe as I had. He shook his head in disbelief, not knowing what to make of it all. We both agreed it was significant.

My last day at the retreat was a tough one. Robert had to depart early in the morning to make the long drive back to his parents' home in Atlanta. He had a six-hour drive ahead of him and still had another two weeks left of his holiday during which he would visit more friends and family. I, on the other hand, was leaving the centre and heading straight back home and back to work. I dreaded the thought of going back to the office.

I watched Robert as he loaded the car with his bags and the kids. Once he had the car packed, it was time to say goodbye. I knew it was going to be hard for me. The three days we'd spent together in Myrtle Beach had intensified our relationship. Seeing the way he interacted with his children, I found him to be a wonderful father, and he was well-liked by the other guests. I hated saying goodbye to him, to Myrtle Beach, to the Meher Baba centre and to my new friends. The notion that I had to leave this Garden of Eden and head back to reality was slowly sinking in. The only thing I was looking forward to was seeing my sons. The only other consolation was that I would catch up with Robert again in a couple of weeks.

I'd made arrangements with Patrick the driver to take me back to the airport later that day. I packed my bag into his car and left the centre with a heavy heart and tears in my eyes. My last day at the centre was 27 June. Patrick and I talked in the car, and he asked me whether I had enjoyed my time. It had been truly magical and memorable, I told him. As we approached the gates that led to the highway, I asked him whether the centre was fully booked for the Fourth of July weekend—a national holiday to celebrate American Independence Day. "Yes, it will be busy, but the next one will be even busier," he said. I calculated that the following weekend would be 10 July. "Why July 10th? What's going on that weekend?" I asked. He looked at me as if to say *don't you know?*

Patrick explained that July 10th was the day Meher Baba began his silence. He was silent from 1925 until his death in 1969. He did not utter a word, choosing instead to use an alphabet board to communicate his messages to the world.

I recalled that Robert had told me about Meher Baba's silence, but I hadn't known 10 July was Silence Day. Then, all of a sudden, it hit me! 10 July was exactly 13 days from now! Thirteen days after my last day in Myrtle Beach! The dream! The Myrtle dream, *Stay Myrtle and after 13 days, see what happens.*

Could this be just another coincidence? The 13th day after leaving Myrtle Beach happened to be the holiest day in Meher Baba's calendar—the day he commenced his silence. It was too much.

Chapter 18

The Silent Voice

Being back home in Australia was so hard. Every now and then, my mind wandered back to the Meher Centre. I could still feel and smell the place. In my mind's eye, I could see the barn, the lake and the lake house. I thought about the fun times and conversations I'd shared with friends in Myrtle Beach. I found myself laughing at some of the conversations we'd had during communal meals.

When Monday came around and I was due back at work, I had a very heavy feeling inside me. I didn't want to go to work. As soon as I stepped into the office, I was hit with the weight of the relentless deadlines and pressures of working in the media. As the morning wore on, I found myself struggling. I sat at my desk wishing I didn't have to be there; on the other hand, I felt guilty, knowing that I just had to get on with things, get back to earning a living and get back to reality. I trawled through all the emails that had mounted up while I was away. Then, just after lunch, I began to feel unwell—so unwell, in fact, that I had to leave the office in the early afternoon. I don't know whether it was psychosomatic or jetlag, but I felt very ill. As soon as I got home, I jumped into bed and feel into a deep sleep.

I woke the following morning with a dreadfully sore throat. I took the rest of the week off work and stayed home to recuperate. My sore throat turned into a chest infection that turned into bronchitis. I eventually lost my voice for three days. I literally couldn't talk, which again brought me back to the dream. The day I lost my voice was Meher Baba's holiest day of the year, Silence Day, 10 July! Unable to talk, I'd been forced to remain silent, even though I had not consciously intended to be silent that day. Robert and I had talked earlier in the week about the upcoming Silence Day. He'd said that out of respect for Meher Baba, he wanted to remain silent for the whole day. I wondered how anyone could do that, given that you would not be able to communicate with anyone, particularly if it fell on a work day. I told him I wasn't sure I could be silent for a whole day. How would I explain it to my children and friends? What would they think if I told them I was adhering to Meher Baba's wishes to remain silent for the day? I could just imagine them wondering what had happened to me in the two weeks I was away. They'd probably think I'd converted to a strange sect or something along those lines.

I wasn't ready to explain myself to everyone just yet, so taking the vow of silence for the day wasn't on the agenda for me. However, because I had lost my voice due to illness, there was nothing to do but remain silent—and nobody questioned me! Silence Day turned out to be a peaceful day, as one would expect. I kept a low profile and spent the day with Robert. My sons were with their father that week, so I didn't have to explain anything to them. I also needed to rest to get over my sore throat and bronchitis. I was concerned about my job, as I'd taken time off for the trip and now another few days because of my illness and loosing my voice.

When I finally returned to work the following Monday, I was keen to catch up with a friend, Therese, who worked on one of the Sunday papers. We arranged to have lunch together. Therese was aware of my Myrtle dream and the reason I'd gone to the US. She was eager to find out what had happened while I was there. I told her about the trip and my opportunity to write an article for *Golfing* magazine. She laughed. I told her about my time at the Meher Baba centre, and I could see her interest pique as I talked about it. "Wow … this is an amazing story," she said. "Would you be able to write a short piece on your dream and why you went to the US? We are featuring a report on spirituality this Sunday. I would like to add your piece to the feature."

This was totally unexpected. I told her that I would love to write it. "How many words and when?" She told me they'd be running the report that coming Sunday so she'd need the story by Wednesday at the latest. And she wanted 300 words. Oh boy, 300 words is very little. I was going to have to tell this tale with the tightest word count! Once again, serendipity was on my side. Here was an opportunity for me to write about the dream, albeit a pared-down version. I was elated at the prospect of sharing my story.

On 17 July 2011, the article appeared. In the back of my mind, I wondered what backlash, if any, I would get from readers. I didn't get any, of course—just some lovely emails from other Meher Baba followers who said they loved hearing the story and that it reminded them that Baba is still very present.

Here's a reproduction of that story.

A Sceptic Embarks on an Inner Journey

by Emily Chantiri – July 17, 2011

As a journalist, I am naturally sceptical of people who try to ram spirituality down my throat.
Yet in March, I had a prophetic dream. I was sitting in a church and a priest approached with a piece of paper saying, "Take this message to the people."
Scribbled on the paper were the words "Stay Myrtle ... And after 13 days see what comes."
Myrtle?
In April, two weeks after my dream, I met a man at a social event. As our friendship developed, I recounted my dream to him and expressed a desire to search for its meaning.
My new friend already seemed to have some clues.
"Have you heard of Myrtle Beach in the US?" he asked, specifying the Meher Baba spirituality centre there. He filled me in on the retreat and revealed that he had plans to be there in June.
Instinctively, I knew this was the "Myrtle" in my dream.
Over the years, I've received numerous prophetic dreams and messages. Instinctively, I knew this dream had to do with a book I'd been writing on the power of the inner voice.
I discovered that Meher Baba, an Indian spiritual master, died in 1969. His followers come from all over the world to share in his philosophies on life, love and service to others.
In June, I made the decision to fly to Myrtle Beach. While at the Meher centre, I spent time learning about Meher Baba's teachings and reaffirmed the idea behind my book. Also, I discovered another Meher centre in Woombye, Queensland. Incidentally, "Woombye", an aboriginal word meaning "black myrtle", further confirmed this was the "Myrtle" in my dream. The journey is far from over.

Chapter 19

Getting Back to Normal

The daily grind of work was really getting to me. I'd spent the last five years writing for a business publication, and I knew the time had come for me to move on. Halfway through 2011, I decided I would leave my job when the time was right, and that it would definitely be later that same year. Following the appearance of my "Myrtle" article in the Sunday paper, I received a number of emails. Most were from Meher Baba followers stating that they'd enjoyed reading the article and, more important, the message in my dream. I thought more about the request I'd received in the dream. *Take this to the people.* This is what the priest in the dream had asked me to do. Perhaps, in a small way, I had done that now. Was my job done? More questions surfaced. I wondered: Did I still need to write a book on intuition?

I'd seriously thought about giving up writing this book, until I began to share my story with friends and colleagues and discovered they wanted to know more about the outcome of the dream. Many urged me to write my story. A friend of mine, Rose, said, "People are after this information. This story will help others follow their instincts." She encouraged me to continue writing the book. The book also gave me another reason to leave my job. If I left, I'd have the time to dedicate to working on my personal projects, including this book. I'd finished revising the second edition of *Savvy Girl's Money Book*, which was due to relaunch in January 2012. This meant I would have even more time to focus on other projects.

In December 2011, I resigned from my job, feeling confident that I'd made the right decision. The media industry was going through massive changes, largely due to newspapers becoming more web-focused. Many readers were now accessing news digitally, and this had impacted sales of print-format papers and magazines. About six months after I left my job, the company was offering major redundancies to my former colleagues and staff. I never had any doubt that I'd made the right decision to leave. Before I left, I'd planned to remain as a contributor to the papers as well as to other publications. Freelance writing was where I needed to be, even though it was going to be challenging. Finally, I'd made time to write and to keep a promise to finish this book. I followed my intuition, and to this day, I am still writing about business, finance and management, and I also write a few health-related articles now and then.

Which leads me to today and to the remainder of my story …

Chapter 20

Life Goes On

It's been more than two years since I had the dream that set me off on a journey. My relationship with Robert continues, and he is very much a part of my life. I still haven't made the trip to India, because I still haven't felt the need. Everything about this journey has been based on intuition. And intuitively, it's not the time to go to India just yet.

I've often thought about those words that came to me in the dream: *"Stay happy and content."* I used to strive for happiness in my life, but today I strive for contentment. Sure, it's great to be happy, but happiness is about wanting this thing or that thing, whereas contentment is accepting where you are and what you have. If you're striving to be happy all the time, you are playing a game that you can never win, because happiness depends on external factors that change from moment to moment. You may be happy one minute, but the reality is you can just as easily fall into the opposite of happy, and that's unhappy!

Contentment is a place you can be in all the time. Contentment is not reliant on having something or doing anything. When you are content, you accept the changes in your life and ride them like waves. Sometimes the waves are stormy, and sometimes they're calm. That's life. Learning to ride the stormy days and enjoy them as much as the calm, peaceful days has provided me with a far greater richness to my life. That richness is largely due to the dreams I've had that have led me to follow my intuition on a daily basis.

Everyone will have their path to contentment. For me, the road of contentment has led me to a spiritual path. This path has enriched my life in many ways. I never thought I would write a book about intuition. As I've said, I'm certainly no expert, and I don't have any special gifts that other people don't have. For me, intuition is a gift that we *all* have. By learning to tap into it, I believe we can all begin to trust our judgement and have more confidence in our ability to make major decisions.

I'm still unsure why Meher Baba came to me, and I want to reiterate that it's not my intention to convert you to believing that he is the answer to your own contentment and joy. But he has had a profound effect on mine, and for that reason alone, I have mentioned him a number of times in this book. If it hadn't been for my dream, I would never have come across my life partner Robert. I have my intuition to thank for that. I listened to my dream and followed my instincts and had a lot of fun along the way. I had such a strong sense that there was something prophetic about the dream and that, again, was my intuition guiding me. That same dream and strong inner voice led me to discover a spiritual leader who has impacted my life in so many ways. It's not important that anyone else feels connected to Baba the man, but what he says about intuition rings true for me regardless of who he is.

Names have been changed to protect the privacy of individuals.

APPENDIX

The Great Man Himself: Meher Baba

Everyone's experience with spirituality, religion or God is personal. This book isn't about convincing you to become a Meher Baba follower but merely to tell a tale about my spiritual journey, which is still unfolding. We are all on a journey in this life; whether you choose to see it as spiritual is up to you.

I don't consider myself an expert on religion or spirituality. During tough times, I have sometimes turned to God to ask for strength and wisdom. To some, God may seem untouchable; we all have different ideas about what God is. I was brought up Catholic, and for me, that came with an in-built idea that I was connected to God, but I never felt the overwhelming sense of intoxicated love that I felt when I saw Meher Baba. That feeling was—and is—the most powerful I have ever experienced. But I still consider myself to be Catholic, that has never changed.

When my mother died of cancer, she was relatively young, and that tested my belief in God. My mother was hard-working, admired and much loved, and she had a generous heart. When she succumbed to cancer at 51 years old, it was a difficult time for my family. I found myself questioning my faith and asking, Why? Why did she have to die so young?

Why my mother had to die at such a young age is something I still don't understand. Nor do I understand why I was drawn to Meher Baba or why he has appeared in my dreams. As far as I was concerned, I already had God and my own spirituality; I wasn't searching for another religion or guru. That's why I still find this whole connection so profound to this day.

Feeling such a strong and loving connection to Meher Baba, someone I've never even met, was life-changing for me. The overwhelming sense of emotion, which feels like a deep well full of love, is not something I'd ever experienced before. Whatever your spiritual beliefs, Meher Baba was a humanitarian: He taught his followers to love, to respect and to work together. The more I read about him and his teachings on love, respect and humanity, the more I believe this man was beyond human.

An avatar is a deity that takes human form on Earth—a holy person, if you like. People have said that Meher Baba is the avatar of our age. Spiritual ideology states that approximately every 700 years, a new spiritual leader is born. With Meher Baba, this makes sense to me. Other avatars who have come to Earth to teach us throughout the ages include Buddha, Mohammed and Jesus Christ.

The more I learn about Meher Baba, such as his work with the poor, the more love I feel for him. It's a very powerful love. He has given me so much peace of mind and so much strength and comfort since coming into my life. After all, he was the man who coined the phrase, "Do your best, don't worry, be happy, and I will take care of the rest". This has become my mantra.

Whenever I'm struggling or feeling uncertain about something, I bring my thoughts to Baba and his words. And just when I need an answer from him, he always comes through for me.

www.ingramcontent.com/pod-product-compliance
Lightning Source LLC
Chambersburg PA
CBHW070555160426
43199CB00014B/2515